WIN THE JOB & THRIVE IN A MULTIGENERATIONAL WORKPLACE

BY
MARK BEAL,
FRANK KOVACS
KADEER A. PORTER

FOREWORD BY
DAVID PANGILINAN

WIN THE JOB & THRIVE IN A MULTIGENERATIONAL WORKPLACE

BY
MARK BEAL,
FRANK KOVACS
KADEER A. PORTER

Published by Mark Beal Media, LLC
Toms River, New Jersey

Cover Design: Nura Hill (www.lightboxlab.design)

ISBN: TBD

First Printing: 2024 Printed in the United States of America

Win The Job & Thrive In A Multigenerational Workplace is available for bulk orders, special promotions and premiums. For details, call Mark Beal at +1.848.992.0391 or email markbeal@markbealmedia.com

DEDICATION PAGE

To my wife, Michele, thank you for inspiring me to pursue my passion projects including this book and to dream big for more than 30 years.

—Mark Beal

To my wife, Laurie, daughter, Julianna, and German Shephard, Rubie, and my parents and in-laws who are kind enough to share me with those I have helped now for 20+ years. Also, the countless volunteers and speakers that help make The Breakfast Club NJ successful!

—Frank Kovacs

To my best friend, my wife, Christina, my mother, Kim, my Aunt Charlene, my fur-baby Bentley, and my entire tribe, thank you for your unwavering motivation and inspiring me to achieve greatness in my own form.

—Kadeer A. Porter

ACKNOWLEDGEMENTS

In 2001, The Breakfast Club NJ (http://www.thebreakfastclubnj.com) was founded by Frank Kovacs to assist individuals in the New York-New Jersey region who were unemployed following the attacks on the United States on September 11, 2001.

We first want to thank The Breakfast Club NJ and other career support networking groups across the United States including, but not limited to, the Professional Services Group (PSG) of Mercer County, Career Support Group at St. Gregory the Great, Professional Service Group of Central New Jersey (PSGCNJ), Monmouth County Division of Workforce Development, and the Philadelphia Area Great Careers Group who are on the front line proactively assisting and supporting individuals who are unemployed and seeking their next opportunity.

We want to thank the thousands of individuals who attend career support networking group meetings like The Breakfast Club NJ. It is your unique career transition journey and proactive mindset to networking and participating in career support group meetings that inspired this book.

We want to thank so many of The Breakfast Club NJ speakers and alums who regularly network and give back in many ways including leading their own career and networking groups including, but not limited to, Benny Recine (St. Gregory The Great), David Schuchman (Professional Services Group Mercer County), Pat Sampson and John Sampson (MIS Networking/ Careers In Transition), Gerry Peyton (Project Management Institute, New Jersey Chapter), Brian Mecca (Comp TIA

Association of Information Technology Professionals, Garden State Chapter), Ed Pospesil (Technology Executive Network Group), Alex Freund (Barnes & Nobel Networking Group), Janelle Razzino (Hillsdale Career Resource Network), Paul Licata, James Laverty and Robert Skuba (Lehigh Valley Professionals), John Fugazie (Neighbors Helping Neighbors), Maria Heidkamp (Heldrich Center For Workforce Development, Rutgers University), Rod Colon (Own Your Career), Mary Usher (Professional Services Group Central New Jersey) and Christine Dykeman.

We want to thank David Pangilinan, Manager, Insights and Cultural Intelligence at Paramount for writing the foreword to the book. David represents the innovation, transformation, diversity and inclusion that is taking place in today's multigenerational workplace.

We want to thank Nura Hill for taking our content and transforming it into this published book. Thank you for the time and expertise you dedicated to the layout and design of this book.

Finally, we want to thank all the "givers" in the world. These "givers" are individuals who share their time, support, assistance, counsel and experience to those who are in a career transition and never expect anything in return. It is the "givers" in the world who help those who are unemployed convert opportunities into their next job.

PRAISE FOR WIN THE JOB & THRIVE IN A MULTIGENERATIONAL WORKPLACE

"This book is an amazing resource for what it takes to land a role in a digital disrupted ecosystem, providing a great platform and 360-degree view of landing a role with a focus on emerging trends in the marketplace, soft skill development, multi-channel marketing, succinct preparation and connecting with the multigenerational workforce. There is extensive research done in delivering this content in concise fashion and immense resource categories shared. It is a great ready reckoner for individuals in today's multigenerational workforce to be relevant and play strategically in this competitive workforce and differentiate themselves from the competition."

—Haresh Keswani,
Business Technology Leader

"A definitive guide for post-COVID job searchers and career developers. The authors have fresh insights, honed by constant contact with newbies and veterans alike. Among its themes are that entrepreneurial skills, personal branding, social media and providing thought leadership have greater impact than traditional resumes and references.

This will book will stay close at hand and forever in my library."

—Richard D. Herring (Ret.),
Audible/Amazon
Merrill Lynch Wealth Management,
Educational Testing Service (ETS)

"This book provides readers with many of the keys they need to unlock opportunities in today's job market. It does so by providing insightful lessons on a wide variety of topics, increasing one's awareness of what needs to be done to be seen and valued in the marketplace. The job search process has significantly changed from what it was even a few years ago, so it is especially important to understand what you need to do to put yourself in the best possible position to get the job you want. To summarize, this book will give you practical insights on what you need to do, to not only survive but thrive in this market."

—Gerry Peyton,
IT Risk Director, Prudential Financial

TABLE OF CONTENTS

FOREWORD

By
David Pangilinan

Growing up, I always believed your career was a routine, albeit a simple one, that began once you graduated from college. Then you got married. Then you had kids. Then you bought a home with a backyard so you could have a dog. Maybe even a pool. Then the monotonous, suburban lifestyle would continue.

But the reality is that what I considered to be a monolithic experience for all adults would change the course of my career, and ultimately, my outlook on life. And then I met Mark Beal. As an eager junior at Rutgers University, I wanted to fuel my passion of having a career that required you to be both creative and strategic but was most importantly... fun.

Sitting in a classroom in 2015, Mark's charisma captured my attention. He spoke of campaigns that required cultural finesse, social media posts that needed an understanding of virality, and of trends that needed staying power. I soaked it up. I fell in love with the art and science of public relations. Mark was my north star, he guided me every step of the way, from the very first pen he put onto my resume for internship applications, to writing my letter of recommendation for graduate school at Columbia University.

The search for my role was neither easy nor simple. It was as complex as I was. *Win The Job & Thrive In A Multigenerational Workplace* authored by Mark Beal, technology leader Frank Kovacs, and fellow Rutgers University alum and executive recruiter, Kadeer A. Porter, serves as the perfect tool for those entering the workforce and for those ready for the next step in their respective careers. The dynamic workplace that has evolved at an even faster pace as a result of the pandemic has led to a more competitive landscape where candidates must have the most unique experiences to help them shine against the competition.

Nearly a decade ago, Mark told me to build my passion not just with my "day job," but also with "side gigs," a term I had never heard of before. And I did. I built my social media following, consulted with brands like Google, Samsung, and Hulu, and learned how to apply principles from his classroom to my everyday life. I was able to network myself into internships at companies that as a first-generation, Filipino-American, I would have never believed I could get. I became the face of brands, starred in commercials, and worked with companies to build more culture-forward content. I learned how to negotiate and advocate for myself. I learned how powerful it was to utilize my network. And, most importantly, I learned how important it was to repay the kindness and to "pay it forward."

Today, working at Paramount, overseeing the development of thought leadership studies with audience-forward, culturally fluent insights, I see, live, work and breathe the lessons found in this book. Working with executives and top leadership at Paramount and across the marketing ecosystem, whether it be at company HQ in Times Square or at conferences around the country, I learned how to challenge myself to become more dynamic in the face of adversity, and how dangerous imposter syndrome can be.

Success isn't something that happens overnight, but a race with, not against, yourself to build endurance for what I consider to be the marathon of life. That's what this book, *Win The Job & Thrive In A Multigenerational Workplace*, is all about. It's about learning that life is a continuous cycle of transforming your career and learning that who you become from your experiences is a result of every person you have met, for better or for worse.

Nearly a decade ago, Mark Beal came into my life and jumpstarted my career. Today, whenever he recommends a student or colleague to speak to, I picture myself, a doe-eyed student looking for some meaning in the work. I always take the call. Opportunities can arise in any form, from anyone, and kindness is never forgotten. While I try to avoid speaking in idioms, this one has always rung true for me: "The juice is always worth the squeeze."

Never forget where you started, and always "send the elevator back down."

INTRODUCTION

In 2017, Mark Beal authored *101 Lessons They Never Taught You In College*. The book featured 101 lessons to help Mark's Rutgers University students successfully and seamlessly transition from college to their career. At the conclusion of his classes and by email, Mark would consistently receive questions from his students regarding topics from writing resumes and cover letters to conducting internship and job interviews via phone versus in-person.

Two years later, Mark was invited to speak to more than 80 job seekers who attended a Saturday morning meeting in East Brunswick, New Jersey of The Breakfast Club NJ, a career support networking group. That was the day that Mark met Frank Kovacs who founded The Breakfast Club NJ after the attacks of September 11, 2001 to help many residents of the New York-New Jersey area who were out of work and unemployed. Since 2001, Frank and The Breakfast Club NJ have helped thousands of individuals secure their next job after experiencing unemployment.

While Mark presented to The Breakfast Club NJ, Frank was providing color commentary even though they hadn't rehearsed. Mark delivered his advice to job seekers and Frank built on Mark's job seeking tips by sharing his commentary. Mark delivered recommendations to the job seekers from a marketing perspective and Frank delivered sound technical advice and the two complemented each other incredibly well for the benefit of all the attendees. Less than 24 hours later, Frank and Mark text each other proposing a book idea. The concept for a book to help job seekers experiencing a career transition was born and *Career In Transition* was published in 2020.

The workplace has experienced an incredible transformation in a short period of time since Mark's *101 Lessons They Never Taught You In College* book was published in 2017 and *Career In Transition* co-authored by Mark and Frank was published in 2020. Prior to the arrival of the pandemic in 2020, most executives commuted (in some cases for an hour or more each way) to a physical office building and worked side-by-side with their colleagues from nine-to-five or longer five or more days a week. In many cases, employees spent more time in-person each day with their work family rather than with their real family. Workplace technology was highlighted by conference calls and emails. Working remotely from home for one day in the majority of cases was considered a very special circumstance.

Prior to 2020, the job application and interview processes were fairly traditional. Applicants applied to an open role via a job posting on the company's website or a job board such as Monster. Applicant tracking systems (ATS) were utilized, but many employers relied on a manual review of resumes from job candidates. Other than an initial phone screening with a recruiter in some cases, the majority of interviews were conducted in-person at the employer's office and advanced from a series of one-on-one meetings to a group review. Elements of the interview such as appearance, attire and body language played an influential role. Once hired, new employees onboarded in a traditional in-person manner with face-to-face in-office training and introductions.

Fast forward to 2024 and the workplace looks nothing like it did just five years earlier as a result of the global pandemic as well as other factors such as the "Great Resignation." Many executives now work remotely two or more days a week, something that probably would not have even been considered an option by most employers in 2019. Many companies have exited their large high-rent office settings for less square footage and smaller space that can be used by employees on a rotating basis on the one or two days a week or month when they commute to the office or companies are renting shared space only when needed for client meetings and company gatherings. In-person meetings have given way to Zoom, Teams and other videoconferencing technology. Email, while still in play, has been replaced in part by Slack and direct messaging.

Job postings are now published on many sites including LinkedIn and Indeed as well as on a company's own job board on their website resulting in thousands of applicants for an open position. Candidates now have greater flexibility in applying for jobs that are fully remote or promoted as hybrid. The interview process has transitioned from nearly completely in-person to mostly remote via phone, videoconferencing and other technology in which some candidates do not even engage with a live person but respond to prompts from a robot. Greater emphasis is now placed on voice, articulation, confidence, and mastery of videoconferencing. Once hired, a new employee may be completely onboarded remotely and may never collaborate in person with colleagues for days, weeks, months or even years.

Additionally, many companies today feature an unprecedented five generations of colleagues attempting to collaborate despite their vast differences of experience in the workplace. Members of The Silent Generation (born between 1928-1945), baby boomers (born between 1946-1964), Generation X (born between 1965-1980), millennials (born between 1981-1996) and Generation Z (born between 1997-2012). Ranging from the experienced employees of The Silent Generation in their mid to late 70s to the workplace's newest employees, Gen Z, the oldest of which are ages 21 to 26, an employer's workplace could span 50 or more years. With that comes opportunities and challenges which we will outline in this book.

With these workplace and job application transformations and today's unprecedented multigenerational workforce, Mark and Frank are collaborating on this book, *Win The Job & Thrive In A Multigenerational Workplace*, with one of Mark's former students, Kadeer A. Porter, who is now immersed in executive recruiting. Kadeer not only offers the fresh workplace and recruiting perspective of a Zillennial (someone who is a hybrid of Gen Z and millennial), but Kadeer also introduces the point-of-view of younger generations who are establishing themselves in their careers and aspire to thrive, evolve, and advance.

This book is intended to be a helpful resource for anyone who is seeking his or her next job no matter their age or the circumstance of their unemployment. The book sources job seeking experts as well as testimonials from individuals who offer their job search and workplace advice. It also features all the knowledge and wisdom that Frank has accumulated in leading The Breakfast Club NJ over the past two decades including his incredible strategic approach as well his technical insights coupled with Mark's point-of-view in marketing personal brands and Kadeer's eye-opening insights regarding the job application and recruiting process in 2024 and beyond.

Frank, Kadeer and Mark hope that the 166 lessons in *Win The Job & Thrive In A Multigenerational Workplace* inspire, motivate and energize you whether you are pursuing your next job opportunity or you just started a role with a new employer. Very best wishes for tremendous success on your unique career journey!

PART I

Taking An Innovative Approach
In The New Workplace

BEGIN ANEW

"This is a new year. A new beginning. And things will change."

–Taylor Swift

"Every day is a new beginning," is a popular quote that speaks to optimism and leaving troubles and failures behind. Well, that could not be truer when we look ahead at the future job market. There will never be another time in your career when you will have the opportunity to start anew in this post-pandemic era. *Yale Insights* captured it well in an August 22, 2023, article writing, "The pandemic changed where and how we work, how we think about the place of work in our lives and vice versa – all against a backdrop of rapid technology change, economic upheaval, and a reckoning with racism." The job market of the future will look nothing like the job market of the past several decades. Gone will be the traditional nine-to-five work hours, commuting five days a week to an office building and a reliance on old school tools to communicate and collaborate. The new job market will feature more remote job opportunities than ever before. Work from anywhere (WFA) and a four-day work week will become a more common part of the workplace lexicon. The new workday may be longer than the standard eight-hour shift, but individuals will have greater freedom to manage their work on a schedule that is most conducive for them. Additionally, we believe that we will see many more individuals earn their income via a combination of a full-time job, consulting, side hustles and freelance opportunities and not just one job that they remain at for a decade or more. Innovative employers of the future will encourage their employees, both full and part-time, the opportunity to pursue their passion as a side gig. With this, throw away the employee handbook you have relied on for the past 10 or more years. You can do away with the status quo as the job market is transforming. Now is the time for you to transform and innovate. Now is the time for you to shift your career and workplace paradigm. Start today by establishing your own rules for prospecting companies and job opportunities. This book was written specifically to get you ready to succeed in a new job market. Each of the 166 lessons in this book offers insights to inspire you to test and learn new approaches until you, and only you, determine what the success metrics are for your unique career as we all begin anew.

Brooks, H. (2023, August 22). *Reinventing The Way We Work Again*. Yale Insights. https://insights.som.yale.edu/insights/reinventing-the-way-we-work-again

CHANGE THE RULES

"You are remembered for the rules you break."

–General Douglas MacArthur

In a February 16, 2022, report from Pew Research Center, it reads, "The impetus for working from home has shifted considerably since 2020. Today, more workers say they are doing this by choice rather than necessity." The point is, the rules of the workplace have changed significantly since 2020, and the job candidate/employee should feel empowered to change the rules with respect to how they participate in the job application process and their employment to thrive in their career. Standard approaches to prospecting for a new role prior to 2020 are now antiquated. Like Major Leage Baseball did in 2023 when the league changed several rules to make the game faster and more exciting, job candidates and employees should take a similar approach. We are amid a new era of innovation and transformation where an individual can apply an entrepreneurial mindset and change the rules with respect to the path that they take to secure their next job and the journey they set out on once they begin working in their new role. With consistent advancements in technology and content channels, there are more ways than ever to become a well-informed job candidate and employee. Take control of your unique career journey, including your job search, and set your own rules. Job applicants should no longer rely on the old fashion approach of applying online to a job opening and then crossing their fingers in hopes that they get a response of any kind, even an automated response. Change the rules and don't even apply to the job, at least not initially. Instead, take a proactive and innovative approach to the same destination and begin your job application process by first leveraging your network to identify the recruiter who is leading the job search or someone who knows the recruiter. While that rule-changing approach initially requires a greater investment of time and effort, in the long run, if successfully executed, it will help the candidate bypass the thousands of applicants who are playing by the old rules and taking a reactive approach by simply just applying online for the position. Author Therese Anne Fowler captures it best with her popular quote. "Some old rules are nothing but old habits that people are afraid to change." There is no better time than now to be bold and unafraid – change your habits and the old rules of the workplace, and great things will result.

Parker, K., Horowitz, J. M., & Minkin, R. (2022, February 16). *COVID-19 Pandemic Continue To Reshape Work In America*. Pew Research Center. https://www.pewresearch.org/social-trends/2022/02/16/covid-19-pandemic-continues-to-reshape-work-in-america/

CREATE YOUR OWN RULES

*"Life is about making your own happiness –
and living by your own rules."*

–Aimee Mullins

As a follow-up to the previous lesson, simply don't just change the old rules of the workplace but create and establish your own rules for the workplace. In 2024 and beyond, there are no established rules for your unique career. On the day you graduated high school or college, they didn't give you a diploma and a rule book that guides you throughout your career. The greatest thing about your career is that you get to write the rules. Yes, you create your own rules because you are the one individual who is going to take your unique career journey. There is no better time than now than to establish your own work and career rules as employers are more flexible than ever with key considerations such as workplace location. The sub headline in an August 5, 2023, workplace article in *The Wall Street Journal* claims, "Employers offering flexible work options are hiring at a faster pace than those requiring full-time office attendance." No two career paths are identical and while you will learn from other's experiences, you are on your own career path. As the popular expression goes, "enjoy the journey." You are not even taking the path less traveled. You are building your own career superhighway. In other words, don't put yourself in a box and limit your thinking as it relates to your career. Create your own rules and test new approaches to career development. Flex your entrepreneurial mindset and launch your own startup company. If you have the mindset of setting your own rules for your career, you will go places that no one has ever gone before and that is incredibly energizing and exciting.

Guilford, G. (2023, August 5). *Need To Hire Workers In A Hot Job Market? Let Them Do Some Remote Work*. The Wal Street Journal. https://www.wsj.com/articles/need-to-hire-workers-in-a-hot-job-market-let-them-do-some-remote-work-506f72e6

BUILD YOUR BRAND

"I work on my brand all day from my computer."

–Serena Williams

Now, more than ever, and in the future, your personal brand, including your brand narrative, will be more important in achieving job search success. As companies transitioned to remote and hybrid work locations following the pandemic, employers and hiring managers are conducting more extensive secondary research to identify and vet candidates which means that you need to develop your personal brand in greater detail and articulate and share your brand narrative more extensively than in the past. You first need to recognize that you are a brand just like Google, Amazon and Nike and that your brand requires a compelling and engaging storyline. In *Forbes*, Goldie Chan writes, "In both our look-at-me cultural shift and evolving job market, it's both helpful and necessary to stand out when applying for a job or starting your own company. A personal brand is for (almost) everyone." Your personal brand consists of your past education, career experiences and achievements as well as your values, passions and personality that make you the only you on the planet. If you have never thought about yourself as a brand in the same way as Taylor Swift and LeBron James, it's time to start thinking differently. First, start by taking an audit of your life combining all your personal and professional milestones and highlights. If you are a black belt in karate, leverage that as part of your personal brand narrative. Once you have detailed those milestones, rank and prioritize them in a way that aligns with your future focus. In other words, you first need to have a clear focus on your future career objectives and then leverage and feature your most relevant lifetime milestones, passions, and values as part of our personal brand. With that, you now have the necessary ingredients for your brand narrative and the storytelling you will be conducting via videoconferences and in-person interviews as well as a variety of social and digital channels and platforms. The challenge for you is to now combine those ingredients in a way that results in well organized and logical storytelling that effectively engages all your future critical stakeholders including recruiters as well as allies in your network.

Chan, G. (2018, November 8). *1o Golden Rules Of Personal Branding*. Forbes. https://www.forbes.com/sites/goldiechan/2018/11/08/10-golden-rules-personal-branding/?sh=7475b0bf58a7

THINK & ACT LIKE A MARKETER

"To be in business today, our most important job is to be head marketer for the brand called You."

–Tom Peters

No matter whether you work in finance, accounting, information technology, operations or logistics, starting today, think and act like a marketer. You are the chief marketing officer of your job search and your career. Nobody else is or should be. In a famous column titled, The Brand Called You, author and management expert Tom Peters writes, "To be in business today, our most important job is to be head marketer of a brand called You." While Peters wrote that column more than 20 years ago for *Fast Company*, it is more relevant today following the pandemic than ever before. The pandemic not only ushered in a new job market, but also ushered in a mandate that you need to think and act like a senior marketing executive in addition to your primary profession. Why? First, the job market is more competitive than ever with more individuals seeking their next job. Simply, look back to a few years ago when the "Great Resignation" was at its peak in 2021. Secondly, more companies are becoming increasingly efficient in their staffing and hiring. With that, the job candidate who does the best job in marketing their personal brand will win the job opportunity. Marketing begins well before you receive an invitation for a formal interview. It starts with understanding and developing your personal brand and narrative. It then continues each day in everything you do to market yourself and your brand to get closer to securing your next job. Every phone call you make, meeting you host and thought leadership content you post are all critical elements of a strategic and integrated marketing strategy. You may have never thought this way in the past, but you must think this way moving forward. More importantly, you need to activate these marketing tactics in a highly calculated and proactive manner. Acting and thinking reactively is no longer an option in the new job market. Daily, weekly, and monthly you need to think ahead and develop your marketing strategy and tactics well before you execute them. This marketing-centric approach requires proactive research, preparation, and planning, fully leveraging all your channels (LinkedIn, Instagram, TikTok, blog or podcast) and everyone in your network in a strategically integrated manner.

Peters, T. (1197, August 31). *The Brand Called You*. Fast Company. https://www.fastcompany.com/28905/brand-called-you#:~:text=To%20be%20in%20business%20today,And%20that%20inescapable.

INTERVIEWING AND WORKING IN VIRTUAL SPACES

"Successfully working from home is a skill, just like programming, designing or writing. It takes time and commitment to develop that skill, and the traditional office culture doesn't give us any reason to do that."

–Alex Turnbull

In today's fast-evolving professional landscape, the virtual interview has emerged as a cornerstone of the hiring process, offering both convenience and unique challenges that you can overcome. As the world increasingly turns to remote work and digital connections, mastering the art of virtual interviews has never been more critical. Navigating these digital encounters with confidence and effectiveness demands careful preparation, adaptability, and an understanding of the distinct dynamics at play in the virtual space. Among the most common platforms used for virtual interviews are Zoom, Microsoft Teams, Skype, Google Meet, and Cisco Webex. Remote work and virtual interviews are here to stay. The

National Society of Leadership and Success captures it best by stating, "Since the pandemic, video calls have increased by 50%. In addition, 92% of employees expect to work from home at least once a week and 80% expect to work three days from home." In this chapter, we'll unravel the strategies and insights to help you excel in virtual interviews, ensuring you leave a lasting impression on prospective employers while seizing opportunities in the ever-shifting job market.

Here are some tips on how to successfully navigate and prepare for interviews in virtual spaces:

- Test your equipment: Make sure your computer, microphone, and speakers are working properly. Test your internet connection and make sure it is strong enough to support the video call. Most platforms can be downloaded on a smartphone, so there is no excuse when it comes to utilizing an efficient device.

- Choose a quiet space: Find a place where you will not be interrupted or distracted. Make sure the background is professional and free of clutter.

- Dress professionally: Even though you are not meeting the interviewer in person, it is still important to dress professionally. This will show that you are taking the interview seriously.

- Be on time: Just like a traditional interview, it is important to be on time for your virtual interview. This shows that you are respectful of the interviewer's time.

- Make eye contact: Even though you are not making eye contact with the interviewer in person, it is still important to make eye contact on the screen. This will help you connect with the interviewer and make a good impression.

- Smile: Smiling will help you look more confident and approachable.
- Speak clearly and slowly: It is important to speak clearly and slowly so that the interviewer can understand you. Avoid using slang or jargon.
- Be prepared: Do your research on the company and the position you are interviewing for. Be prepared to answer common interview questions.
- Ask questions: At the end of the interview, be sure to ask questions about the company and the position. This shows that you are interested in the opportunity.
- Use a virtual background: This can help you create a professional setting for your interview. You can also blur your background if the pre-download background doesn't suffice.
- Minimize distractions: Turn off your phone and close any unnecessary applications.
- Be aware of your body language: Even though the interviewer cannot see you in person, it is still important to be aware of your body language. Avoid fidgeting or slouching.

Practice makes perfect and be sure to do so ahead of time. Practice answering common interview questions so that you feel more confident during the actual interview. Benjamin Franklin said it best, "If you fail to plan, you plan to fail." We like to say, "Stay ready so you never have to get ready." You will be better off now, and in the long run!

Author Unknown. (2023, April 5). *How To Make A Good Impression In A Virtual Interview*. National Society of Leadership and Success. https://www. nsls.org/blog/how-to-make-a-good-impression-in-a-virtual-interview

IDENTIFY & TARGET YOUR TOP-20

*"The only way to do great work is to love what you do.
If you haven't found it yet, keep looking. Don't settle.
As with all matters of the heart, you'll know
when you find it."*

–Steve Jobs

Since most job seekers take the traditional approach of waking up each day and scouring the internet for job postings, with this lesson, you now have a way to bypass that old school approach and successfully secure the next opportunity in your career. Applying to job posts is a very traditional job search approach, but the problem is that in the new job market, traditional approaches are no longer going to help you get to where you want to go – the next job in your career. Instead, be innovative and take a non-traditional proactive approach that is required for job searches now and in the future. Once you determine how far you want to commute from where you live (or if you want to work remotely from home), conduct extensive research on every company in that region and identify and rank your top-20 targets. Alison Doyle captures it well when she writes, "With a target list in hand, you will actually save yourself time in your job search. Even if it feels productive to apply to every job opening you come across, you are actually wasting your time and energy. Instead, you should apply only to jobs at companies that you believe are a good fit for you." You will be very surprised to learn of companies you never knew existed, both big and small. Additionally, as you conduct your research and gain insights and intelligence, you will uncover leads and contacts you never knew you had in your personal and professional network. As you identify and build your list of targets, you are only halfway through this process. You now need to audit, analyze and rank the 20 targets you have identified. Ranking these target companies will help you prioritize so that you invest more time in prospecting your top-five targets. How do you rank your targets? Consider a wide variety of factors including connections you have internally (employees) or externally (former employees, vendors), your relevant experience, and anything else you uncovered in your research that makes a company appealing. By ranking your targets, you can now mobilize your followers to help you bypass the online applicant tracking systems and secure an in-person opportunity to meet internal recruiters and other decision makers. This targeting approach to seeking your next job will lead to more success than pushing the send button on an application and hoping you receive a response. Of course, it is most effective when paired with proactive prospecting which we explain in the next lesson. Based on your desired industry and category, as well as the region where you want to live, commute and work or are willing to move to for work, strategically identify and rank as many as 20 or 25 companies and organizations that you would like to make your next home. Of course, this requires more research - research in your region, research about corporate structure and culture and research about employee turnover rates, the vision of the leadership team and any information that indicates that the organization is continuously transforming and keeping pace or ahead of the marketplace and the competition. There will be other reactive opportunities that will come your way, but these 20-25 companies are now your prospects who you are going to strategically and proactively target like you are the world's leading sales representative. Without taking the strategic initiative to research and identify your specific prospects, you are significantly limiting your job search campaign. You would only be employing a reactive approach which means you are simply standing by waiting for the phone to ring or an email to arrive from a potential employer. Now, you have a two-tiered proactive and reactive sales prospecting approach that will significantly expedite the journey to the next destination in your career.

Doyle, A. (2020, July 22). *Build Your Employer Target List*. Live About. https://www.liveabout.com/build-your-employer-target-list-2059435

PERFECT PROACTIVE PROSPECTING

"I like to encourage people to realize that any action is a good action if it's proactive and there is positive intent behind it."

–Michael J. Fox

"There are job opportunities available today, experts say, but job seekers may need to take a different approach to finding their next career move than they have in the past," writes Beth Braverman for CNBC. That different approach that Braverman highlights is what we call proactive prospecting. Now that you have researched and ranked your top-20 targets as discussed in the previous lesson, your strategic and proactive prospecting begins. Instead of waiting for these 20 companies to post a job that you qualify for, you are going to prospect your target companies in a way that potentially may enable you to avoid formally applying. How? This is where your personal and professional network plays a role. In proactively prospecting, your mission is to mobilize your network with the goal of identifying one individual in your network who has just one substantive connection with one of the 20 target companies you are prospecting... and do that 20 times. Of course, some of your contacts may have strong connections with more than one of your 20 targets. Michael Klazema explains why we take this prospecting approach when he writes for Professionals For Nonprofits Staffing Group, "According to the University of Michigan University Career Center, referrals account for just 7% of all job applicants, but 40% of all hires. In other words, having someone in your corner who can put in a good word with the hiring manager will drastically improve your chances of getting hired." Once you start to identify contacts who have solid connections with someone affiliated with your targeted companies, you then need to proceed to the next phase, having your contact reach out to their contact and request an informational interview on your behalf. As those interviews are placed on the calendar, you need to prepare for the all-important phase three of proactive prospecting, acing the informational interview. While it may be positioned as an informational interview to your audience, to you, it is the opportunity to demonstrate the business-building value you can deliver. In the process, you want to engage, impress, and motivate the interviewer enough to go the extra step and introduce you to an in-house recruiter or human resources executive for consideration for current or future openings. That type of endorsement and advocacy is something you will never earn from a traditional reactive job search mindset and approach.

Braverman, B. (2020, May 28). *Laid Off During The Pandemic? Honing These Skills Can Boost Your Job Prospects.* CNBC. https://www.cnbc.

com/2020/05/28/laid-off-during-the-pandemic-honing-these-skills-boosts-job-prospects.html

Klazema, M. (2016, October 18). *8 Ways You Can Increase Your Chances Of Getting Hired*. Professionals For Nonprofits Staffing Group. https://pnpstaffinggroup.com/8-ways-can-increase-chances-getting-hired/

DEVELOP YOUR JOB SEARCH TOOL

"You miss 100% of the shots you don't take."

–Wayne Gretzky

One of the ways of going beyond your traditional resume is to create a simple one-page job search tool. While a resume is required for job applications, it only captures your past education, experiences, and achievements. You need to develop a job search tool to empower your network to help you get to where you want to be in the future. In meeting with the contacts in your network to share and discuss your 20 target companies, a resume is not going to be very helpful. Your job search tool is going to serve as the instructions for how your network can assist you in the most efficient and effective manner possible. How? Again, your resume represents your past. Your job search tool shares your vision for your future. No matter how you design your one-page job search tool, there are three core areas. The first section features your contact information along with how far you are willing to commute from the location of your home residence or if you are only seeking remote employment. That commutation distance is very important as it creates the geographic region for your job search and your contacts need to know that. The second section lists the type of titles you are seeking. For example, if you are a seasoned marketing executive, your network contacts need to know if you are only pursuing jobs with titles of chief marketing officer or if you are also interested in opportunities at the director and vice president levels. Last, but not least, is the most important section. This third section lists the 20 or more companies that you have researched, identified, and ranked as your targets. This is where this job search tool delivers significantly more value than a resume. It's when you get to this third section that your allies clearly understand the companies where you are looking to secure a job. Your ask to your contacts is to simply identify one contact at just one of your 20 target companies and then make a request on your behalf for an informational interview. If you can successfully achieve that with 20 of your contacts, your job search tool just opened the door for you to 20 companies where you want to work. That is something you resume can't do. More importantly, it is something that gets you one major step closer to employment at a company and corporate culture where you want work and thrive. "One of my much admired mentors told me this one pager was critical to my search for two reasons: 1) it will help you focus on what it is that you truly want with your next professional role and 2) it will help your network effectively and efficiently advocate on your behalf when recommending you to their network," commented PJ Brovak, a marketing communications veteran.

ESTABLISH YOUR KPI'S

*"Do not measure success by today's harvest.
Measure success by the seeds you plant today."*

–Robert Louis Stevenson

While your ultimate goal is to secure a job with one of your target companies, you need to establish key performance indicators (KPIs) or metrics for success to measure your progress on a daily, weekly, monthly and quarterly basis. Without KPIs, you are randomly beginning each day with little or no focus. Hannah Morgan describes it best in an article she wrote for *US News & World Report*, "The ultimate measure of your success in job search is a job offer. However, in order to reach this goal, you have to take the right actions and track your outcomes. It's hard to know how to adjust your job search if you don't know what works for you." It is also challenging to measure outcomes if you have not established measurable action-oriented objectives. Of course, these KPIs should adhere to the SMART goal formula – Specific, Measurable, Achievable, Realistic, Timebound. Based on a few previous lessons in this book, one KPI should focus on making substantive inroads and quality introductions at each of your 20 target companies. The KPI can state: Mobilize my network and make internal connections at two of my target companies each week for 10 weeks. That KPI is specific, measurable, achievable, realistic and timebound. By establishing it, you now have something substantive and tangible to work against each week. After the first week, you may learn that the KPI is too ambitious, and you need to adjust it to making one internal connection each week at just one target company. Without this type of KPI, you have no way to evaluate your progress or the motivation and incentive to accomplish the many goals you will need to achieve on your path to securing your next job.

Morgan, H. (2016, June 1). *8 Ways To Measure Job Search Success*. US News & World Report. https://money.usnews.com/money/blogs/outside-voices-careers/articles/2016-06-01/8-ways-to-measure-job-search-success

TRACK & MEASURE
YOUR PROGRESS

"Measuring progress is often like watching grass grow. While it's difficult to detect movement on a daily basis, it's simple to see growth over time."

–Frank Sonnenberg

Once you have established your customized list of KPIs as discussed in the previous lesson, have them work harder for you by tracking and measuring your progress weekly. In an article titled, 12 Ways To Measure Your Job Search Progress, Barb Poole writes, "Every Sunday, evaluate the prior week and plan the coming week." For example, if one of your KPIs is to meet one new person each day who can assist you in your job search, that's seven new meaningful connections each week. By tracking against that KPI, on Sunday, you can measure very efficiently how you are performing against that specific metric. You can simply do this by using an excel chart or customizing your own tracking mechanism that works well for you and your preferred approach. Measurement will inform you if a KPI is too ambitious or if you have set the bar too low. All of a sudden, by establishing that one KPI and tracking and measuring your progress, your job search has taken a more strategic approach than the vast majority of job seekers which ultimately puts you in a much better position to win the job. The key is to track and measure a robust set of KPIs that have been developed specifically for you and your unique career journey. Weekly, you should also be measuring the number of informational interviews, formal interviews as well as your content creation, distribution and engagement as measuring all of these KPIs will confirm what is working well and inform how you need to course correct in the week ahead.

Poole, B. (n.d.). *12 Ways To Measure Your Job Search*. Acendance. https://acendance.com/job-search/12-ways-measure-job-search-progress/

OWN & LEVERAGE YOUR MEDIA CHANNELS

"Content builds relationships."

–Andrew Davis

In an earlier lesson, we wrote that you need to think and act like a marketer. This lesson builds on that recommendation. If you were a marketer for a consumer brand like Nike or Taco Bell, part of your role as chief marketing officer is to fully leverage your owned media channels. Your owned media channels are all your online platforms – LinkedIn, Facebook, Instagram, TikTok – that you own, manage and ultimately determine the content that gets produced and distributed. You don't need to pay for advertising on these channels and you don't have to pitch an editor to write a story. You own these channels and platforms, but up until now, you probably have not fully leveraged their combined power and influence. Cheryl Lock writes, "Build a strong social media profile that catches the attention of recruiters. Use LinkedIn and other platforms to create and display a professional profile that's frequently updated with information about your professional assets." During the pandemic, many of us were introduced to channels like Zoom and quickly mastered these channels. Now, do the same with channels where you already have a presence, but have not leveraged. LinkedIn is a perfect example. Most professionals create a LinkedIn profile with a photo and a list of experience and education and leave it at that. They grew up in an older job market where there was a philosophy of, "build it and they will come." In today's marketplace, where recruiters are conducting as much research to identify candidates as you are doing to identify job openings, you need to take greater ownership of an owned media channel like LinkedIn and utilize it as your own content distribution platform. In addition to building the framework for your profile, today, you need to build and maintain the 24-hour news engine that is going to drive engagement on your LinkedIn page.

Lock, C. (n.d.). *How To Create A Personal Brand That Enhances Your Job Search*. Flejobs. https://www.flexjobs.com/blog/post/how-to-create-a-personal-brand-to-enhance-your-job-search-v2/

BE A THOUGHT LEADER

"Thought leadership is by nature evolutionary,
in that it must always be part of an ever-evolving flow."

–Pearl Zhu

Now that you have read the previous lesson and realize that you own your media channels, but you are not letting them work hard and smart enough for you, it's time to become a thought leader. Aside from LinkedIn, which over the past several years has evolved into a substantive thought leadership content sharing hub, consider creating your own blog, web site and even a podcast. In today's world of virtual teleconferencing, producing, hosting, and distributing a podcast is something that can be accomplished efficiently as you adopt, learn and utilize new technologies and skills. We are not going to provide a tutorial here on how to build your own website, blog, or podcast. More importantly, it is what you do with all your owned media channels. Based on the elements and values that comprise your personal brand and the components of your brand narrative, you need to emerge as a thought leader in the profession and industry where you have set your sights. Thought leadership is the process of researching, writing, producing, and distributing your point-of-view on topics relevant to your profession and industry. A strategic thought leadership distribution strategy could feature one piece of content that originates on your blog and is amplified via LinkedIn and even Facebook. You could take the same topic and explore it in audio form on your podcast with a guest who can provide commentary. This strategic approach to thought leadership helps you achieve three things that are critical to your strategic search. First, it raises your online profile and your brand in a way that can't be done via an old school word-of-mouth campaign. Secondly, it leads to engagement and collaboration with others in your profession including job recruiters and human resources departments. Finally, it reinforces everything you articulate via your brand narrative in informational and formal interviews. Hiring decision makers will read and review your thought leadership following your interview. It should not only impress them, but it could very well be the deciding factor between you and another candidate who has published limited or no thought leadership content.

SUCCEED WITH SEO

"No matter how niche or mainstream your market is, great content remains a significant focus for SEO."

–Kristopher Jones

"**B**oosting the SEO of your blog, website and social media presence will allow recruiters and candidate-searching employers to more easily and quickly discover you; and while of course you should also be applying to jobs and networking within your industry, better SEO means a higher chance of naturally attracting interested visitors," writes Jon Simmons for Monster.com. Now that you understand that you need to fully leverage your owned media channels with compelling and engaging thought leadership content, it's critically important to boost your SEO (search engine optimization) to continue to raise your online profile and presence. We discussed producing and publishing thought leadership content. That's the first step in boosting your SEO. Without publishing thought leadership content, there is nothing to boost. Next, you can't make the mistake that many individuals and even brands make. They launch their thought leadership content in a flurry only to quickly fade away. Another key to boosting SEO is to consistently produce and distribute thought leadership content. Don't attempt to do too much too soon. Instead, as part of your success metrics that we discussed in an earlier lesson, set a manageable goal of authoring and distributing one piece of content each week consistently. If you determine that you can increase it to two times a week, that is fine, but again, it needs to be consistent. Finally, as Simmons writes, "Get the metadata right." He explains, "Keywords matter because they help search engines identify content on your site, as well as the content on your social media posts, and increases their search ranking. Working keywords specific to your desired job or industry into page titles, meta descriptions, articles, tweets, ups your shot at getting discovered through Google."

Simmons, J. (n.d.). *Here's How To Boost Your Job Search SEO*. Monster. https://www.monster.com/career-advice/article/how-to-boost-your-job-search-seo-and-why-you-need-it-to-get-hired

WATCH MORE WEBINARS

*"Online learning is not the next big thing,
it is the now big thing."*

–Donna J. Abernathy

Conduct a simple Google search using the term, "webinars for job seekers," and immediately right at your fingertips you will have hundreds of hours of content to download and view. Since the arrival of the pandemic, webinars have become the norm, not the exception. While webinars may lack the in-person connection and collaboration you can find at a career support networking group meeting, webinars offer a wide variety of other advantages. First, from the comfort of your home, you can easily log in or download a webinar at any time that is convenient for you. Second, webinars offer information and inspiration on every topic related to seeking your next opportunity for employment including, but not limited to, The New Rules of Modern Job Search, Network Yourself To A Great Career, How To Write A Stand-Out Resume, Creating A Value Added Resume and even, Beating Applicant Tracking Systems. Finally, most webinars are free and feature experts offering advice and counsel in their area of expertise regarding careers and job search. As you get more comfortable with remote learning, expand your horizons and take in some employment focused TEDx Talks including Jason Shen's "Looking For A Job? Highlight Your Ability, Not Your Experience," or Regina Hartley's "Why The Best Hire Might Not Have The Perfect Resume" and Ashwini Mrinal Bhagat's "What I Learned From 32 Grueling Interviews." There are no longer any excuses for job seekers if you have access to the internet from your laptop or phone.

RECRUIT RELATIONSHIPS REMOTELY

*"I consider the most important job of someone
like myself as recruiting."*

–Steve Jobs

Shortly after the pandemic arrived in the United States, Vicky McKeever of CNBC wrote, "Dr. Rosina Racioppi, CEO of professional development program provider Women Unlimited, believed that social distancing and the coronavirus could be a catalyst for increased online networking... Reaching out to existing and new contacts on LinkedIn is one method suggested by Racioppi." The global pandemic ushered in a new chapter in professional networking. While conferences and in-person meetings have returned, remote relationship building is here to stay which means individuals are much more receptive to inquiries from you, a job seeker who has value to offer. Why? Employers and employees understand that working remotely offers several advantages including the elimination of commuting to work and other efficiencies. These efficiencies lead to more time for those who are employed to connect and collaborate, which is something you must leverage. In their May

2020 edition, *AARP Bulletin* highlights, "Contacts are critical in what may be a highly competitive post-coronavirus job market. Methodically extend your circle. Join online professional groups for networking on LinkedIn and Facebook. Touch base with former colleagues and classmates." There is no better time than now to network and recruit relationships remotely. Those may be entirely new relationships or former colleagues and classmates who you have lost contact with. It is more common and acceptable today to network and connect with professionals via LinkedIn and even sending a direct message through Instagram or another social media platform, so fully leverage the relationship-building channels and platforms that are at your fingertips.

Hannon, K. (2020a, May 5). *How You Can Prepare Yourself For The New Job Market*. AARP. https://www.aarp.org/work/careers/coronavirus-changing-job-market/

McKeever, V. (2020, March 20). *How To Become Better At Networking Despite The Coronavirus Keeping You At Home*. CNBC. https://www.citationmachine.net/apa/cite-a-website/custom

PRIORITIZE THE REMOTE JOB MARKET

*"People are more productive working at home
than people would have expected."*

–Mark Zuckerberg

The June 2020 edition of *AARP Bulletin* wrote it best so we will let them lead this lesson. "Large employers such as Dell, SAP and UnitedHealth Group are among the top 100 remote-friendly companies, recently culled from a database of 54,000 employers by FlexJobs. Even as unemployment skyrocketed during the pandemic and the outbreak threatened a mass recession, UnitedHealth, based in Minnetonka, Minnesota, was looking to fill over 200 remote positions in every part of the company." The story quotes Richard Johnson of the Urban Institute. "We've learned from the pandemic that many kinds of workers can work from home. Both employees and employers are learning that new technologies make remote working easy and productive. Those lessons won't be forgotten once the pandemic ends." *The Wall Street Journal* echoed this sentiment on August 5, 2023, with a workplace article featuring the headline, "Need to Hire Workers in a Hot Job Market? Let Them Do Some Remote Work." What does this mean for you? While your job search should be strategic, proactive, and focused, you no longer have to limit your search to companies that are physically located in your desired region to commute from home. You can now expand your search to companies that are increasing their number of remote work positions. This means that you need to shift and expand your search and your mindset to job opportunities beyond those that are exclusively located in old school physical office buildings to the thousands of new jobs that are part of the burgeoning remote job market. For many who commuted for many years to an office, this is an exciting new frontier in the job market and one that you should leverage to your advantage.

Guilford, G. (2023b, August 5). *Need To Hire Workers In A Hot Job Market? Let Them Do Some Remote Work*. The Wall Street Journal. https://www.wsj.com/articles/need-to-hire-workers-in-a-hot-job-market-let-them-do-some-remote-work-506f72e6?mod=business_lead_pos7&utm_source=briefing&utm_medium=email&utm_campaign=brands_am&utm_content=080723

Hannon, K. (2020, June 9). *5 Reasons Working From Home Benefits Older Workers - And Their Employers*. AARP. https://www.aarp.org/work/careers/telework-benefits/

THINK & ACT LIKE A ZEO

"As the first generation to grow up with smartphones, social media, and remote work... the world will see this ambitious group is boundless."

–Jesse Kay

For those who are unaware, Generation Z (Gen Z) is comprised of any individual who was born starting in 1997 through 2012. By 2030, it is projected that at least 30 percent of the workforce will be comprised of members of Gen Z. The oldest Gen Zers graduated from high school and college and joined the workforce. We like to call these newest entrants to the workplace, ZEOs. Jacqueline Parkes, the former chief marketing officer of MTV, described Gen Z best when she proclaimed, "Gen Z is the first generation that swiped before they wiped." While humorous, Jacqueline's quote captures this cohort well. Gen Z has had technology in their hands since a very early age and they use technology to their advantage especially when it comes to their job search and work. Our advice, if you have a Gen Z child or a nephew or niece who is in college or recently graduated, schedule some quality time with them to strategize. You will be amazed how much you will learn from someone in their early 20s. As it relates to your job search, they will teach you about apps, programs and web sites that will assist you. They will probably also be able to share some tips on how to fully leverage LinkedIn and how to evolve your thought leadership content production and distribution. Also known as the "purpose generation," members of Gen Z are eager to lend their support and assistance to a worthy cause. Your job search qualifies as a worthy cause for any Gen Zers who are close relatives of yours. Diversity and inclusion are a priority of employers in response to the Black Lives Matter awakening. Before you conduct your next job interview, spend some time with one or more Gen Zers and truly understand what diversity and inclusion means, why it is a priority in their lives and why employers will most likely gauge your point-of-view on this very important topic the next time you speak to a recruiter. It's all about becoming more informed, educated, and aware. If you are a member of Gen Z seeking your next career opportunity, fully leverage your tech acumen, digital savviness, and entrepreneurial mindset to your advantage as you network, prospect for jobs, engage with recruiters and conduct job interviews.

EMBRACE THE LATEST TECHNOLOGY & TRENDS

"Good, bad or indifferent, if you are not investing in new technology, you are going to be left behind."

–Philip Green

For as long as we can remember, human civilization continues to progress to new heights, especially when it comes to technology and processes. Corporations like Apple, Microsoft, and Google control most of everything we use to live our lives on the most basic level. Drone technology, once only used by official government agencies and military personnel, has been made available in different industries such as sports, film and photography, construction, real estate, and so much more. If you want to achieve success and continue to be a game-changer, you must be able to embrace new technology and trends. The COVID-19 pandemic has accelerated the development and adoption of new technologies and trends, and all generations understand that more than ever before. Some of the most notable new technologies and trends that have emerged in the post-COVID world include:

Artificial intelligence (AI): AI is being used in a wide variety of industries, from healthcare to customer service. AI can be used to automate tasks, make predictions, and improve decision-making.

Blockchain: Blockchain is a secure and transparent way to store data. It is being used in a variety of applications, such as cryptocurrency and supply chain management.

Big Data: Big Data is the collection and analysis of large amounts of data. It can be used to identify trends, make predictions, and improve decision-making.

Internet of Things (IoT): The IoT refers to the network of physical devices that are connected to the internet. These devices can collect and share data, which can be used to improve efficiency and operations.

Virtual reality (VR): VR is a technology that allows users to experience a simulated environment. It is being used in a variety of applications, such as gaming, education, and healthcare.

Augmented reality (AR): AR is a technology that superimposes a computer-generated image on a user's view of the real world. It is being used in a variety of applications, such as gaming, education, and retail.

5G Connectivity: The arrival of 5G networks heralds a new era of connectivity, offering unprecedented speeds, minimal latency, and expanded network capacity. This groundbreaking technology is poised to reshape various industries, including telecommunications, healthcare, autonomous vehicles, and immersive experiences like augmented reality (AR) and virtual reality (VR).

These are just a few of the many new technologies and trends that have emerged in the post-COVID world. As these technologies continue to develop, it is important to stay up-to-date and embrace them. Abubakar Zaidi emphasizes the importance of staying updated stating, "By staying abreast of these trends, we can embrace the opportunities they offer and contribute to a future where technology continues to enhance our lives in profound ways." Here are some specific tips for embracing the latest technology and trends:

- Read industry publications and blogs: This is a great way to stay up to date on the latest trends and developments.

- Attend industry events: This is a great way to network with other professionals and learn about new technologies and trends.

- Take online courses and workshops: This is a great way to learn about new technologies and trends in a hands-on way.

- Experiment with new technologies and trends: The best way to learn about a new technology or trend is to try it out for yourself.

- Be open to change: The world of technology is constantly changing, so it is important to be open to change and new ideas.

These tips are extremely helpful for navigating in the now. We will continue to create breakthrough technology that allows us to be more efficient in the workplace, but this is only the beginning. Keep your finger on the pulse and challenge yourself to always remain curious. Do this and you won't be left behind.

Zaidi, A. (2023, July 12). *Embracing The Future: Exploring The latest Trends In Technology*. Medium. https://medium.com/@ma2003110/embracing-the-future-exploring-the-latest-trends-in-technology-5f1a9f9d910

NEVER STOP LEARNING

"Live as if you were to die tomorrow. Learn as if you were to live forever."

–Mahatma Gandhi

No matter how much experience you have, you will never be able to learn enough for any future job opportunity. In other words, never stop learning. Each and every day, learn something new about the industry, company or job you are targeting. You can start by reading the detailed job qualifications for the types of jobs and the level at which you aspire to work. In fact, use those published job postings as your checklist and review each qualification and then determine which ones you need to secure. It could be something as significant as going back to school to earn your graduate degree or it could be a certificate in a specific skill area that you can study and receive in a few weeks via online courses and testing. In *Forbes*, Robin Ryan explained it best when she wrote, "Do not just sit around and waste time. If you are unemployed, getting new skills is a very wise idea. Decide on one professional thing you can work on to improve your skillset. You can use your library card (or signup online for a free one) and go to Lynda.com. You'll find hundreds of free classes available courtesy of your local library. These are high-quality programs that will teach you professional skills, business skills, and help you with technology if you need it. In a month, you could master something if you spent just one hour a day studying it." The pandemic gave many of us the gift of time forced to work and socialize from home. Continue to use that that time to your advantage especially to work against that checklist of qualifications that you need to secure to have any chance at winning the job at that company and in that industry where you have set your sights.

Ryan, R. (2020, April 2). *Unemployed? How To Use This Time Wisely*. Forbes. https://www.forbes.com/sites/robinryan/2020/04/02/unemployed-how-to-use-this-time-wisely/?sh=291a82bb4954

GOOGLE YOURSELF

"Knowing yourself is the beginning of all wisdom."

–Aristotle

As you proactively prospect for jobs at the companies and organizations you have strategically researched and identified, put yourself in the mindset of the recruiter. If they like what they see after they receive and review your resume, the next logical step they will take is to Google you to uncover anything that you may have left out of your resume while confirming what you highlighted. They have just transformed themselves from an executive recruiter to a detective. In a *Glassdoor* article, it was written, "When applying for a job, you're really giving a relative stranger permission to stalk you online. In fact, 90 percent of hiring managers use Google search results when considering executive hires, according to 2012 research from ExecuNet." We are fairly certain that the 90 percent number is probably closer to 100 percent in 2024 and beyond. With that, Google yourself and discover what the recruiter will discover. Is it positive or will it eliminate you from the competition before you even get the chance to conduct your first interview? If you do not like what you see, take ownership and produce and distribute thought leadership content across your owned media channels with a focus on LinkedIn. Additionally, finally create that blog that you have been considering for years and use that as a strategic platform to share relevant and meaningful content that will engage a recruiter. Aside from the written word, Google yourself to learn what images a recruiter might see. If you don't like what you see, invest a few dollars in professionally photographed images and then feature the new image that you believe is your best across all your channels so that it appears in future searches. The key to this lesson is to shift your mindset from the job applicant to the job recruiter. If you are able to do that, you will discover a wealth of content that needs to be updated to improve your chances the next time you impress someone with your resume.

Clean Up Your Google Search Results Before Applying For A Job - Here's How. Glassdoor. (2018, April 10). https://www.glassdoor.com/blog/ clean-up-google-search-results-before-applying-for-a-job-heres-how/#:~:text=Google%20Yourself%20When%20Applying%20 For%20a%20Job&text=When%20searching%20your%20 name%2C%20sign,to%20see%20what%20strangers%20see.

OUTHUSTLE & OUTSMART THE COMPETITION

"It doesn't take ability to hustle."

–Joseph Hooks

Not only are you actively seeking your next employment opportunity, but you are competing against many more candidates for every single position you apply for. In a *Time* article on June 14, 2023, the author writes, "Part of the difficulty stems from a tightening labor market especially from fields like tech that have had hundreds of thousands of layoffs in the last nine months. There is now, on average, one job opening for every two applicants on LinkedIn, a big change from early 2022, when there was one job opening per applicant on average." So, what do you do? You need to rachet up all your efforts. You need to outhustle and outsmart the competition. Simply applying to jobs via an online portal and applicant tracking system is no longer going to cut it in 2024 and beyond. You need to face every day like it is the World Cup, Olympic Games, Super Bowl, World Series and NBA Championship all rolled into one. Your full-time job now is to secure your next full-time job and if that requires a 24/7 mindset and effort, that is exactly what you need to do because your competition, the one that is going to win the next job you apply for, has already been proceeding with that 24/7 mindset. There has been an increasingly popular mantra the past few years from successful executives who like to tell their mentees and followers, "work smarter, not harder." When it comes to securing your next job, we are urgently recommending you to, "work smarter and harder." That is how you will beat the unprecedented number of competitors who are between you and your next job.

Senuels, A. (2023, June 14). *You're Not Imagining It-Job Huntong Is Getting Worse*. Time. https://time.com/6287012/why-finding-job-is-difficult/

NEVER FINISH WRITING
YOUR RESUME

*"Life is our resume. It is our story to tell,
and the choices we make write the chapters."*

–Matthew McConaughey

If you are of the mindset now as you seek your next job opportunity that all you need to do is blow the dust off your old resume and add your most recent experience, you are sorely mistaken. First, starting today, commit to the concept that you will never finish writing your resume. In other words, your resume is a living document that should modified and customized every time you apply to a new job position. Kim Isaacs writes, "Submitting the same resume for every position can't possibly meet each employer's individual requirements. If you want to grab the hiring managers' attention, you need to give them what they want. You must take the time to tailor your resume to each employer and its goals to strengthen your chances of getting noticed." Your journey to your next job is not a competition in speed. You do not earn points or win the job by being the person who applies fastest or applies to more job openings than anyone else. Start to think less like the rabbit and more like the tortoise. Begin to prioritize quality over quantity in everything you do as part of your search. For example, it is not about quickly meeting 10 new people this week, but rather, engaging, collaborating, and launching mutually beneficial relations with one or two new people weekly. That brings us back to your resume. Take your time and develop and detail a high-quality resume that will serve as your foundation. Once you believe you have established that quality foundation, share your resume with those in your network who you trust and let them poke holes and make revisions and edits. Now, you have a resume that will serve as the quality foundation you need to continuously evolve and customize for each individual job you apply to. The key as you apply is to ensure the quality of your resume does not diminish while you customize specific terms and language that align with the job description and qualifications for the job you are applying.

Isaacs, K. (n.d.). *Customize Your Resume For Best Results*. Monster. https://www.monster.com/career-advice/article/customize-your-resume-for-results

DON'T LEAVE YOUR EGO AT HOME

"Believe in yourself! Have faith in your abilities! Without a humble but reasonable confidence in your own powers, you cannot be successful or happy."

–Norman Vincent Peale

In having conducted hundreds of job interviews and mock interviews, we have found that it is very common for the interviewee to downplay their accomplishments and achievements. First, they don't want to come off as boastful. Second, because they achieved something special in the past, they somehow have convinced themselves that it can't be a truly impressive achievement. There is no better time than now while you are immersed in a highly competitive job market to as Daniel Bortz calls it, "humblebrag." He writes, "Great interviews are all about selling yourself to an employer. The hiring manager has seen your resume. She knows what you're like on paper. Now you've got to close the deal. Naturally, this means highlighting your achievements. But when you're in the hot seat, do you suddenly get bashful, and worry that you'll sound like a big bragger when talking about your career or educational accomplishments? Don't. That's what you're there for." We recommend, "be confident, not cocky." Whether on your resume, an informational interview, or a formal final interview, don't hold back. You only have one chance to make a strong lasting impression. You cannot go back the next day and retake the final exam. As you conduct your audit of all your accomplishments and achievements to develop your brand narrative as discussed in a previous lesson, consider everything. If you are already 10 or more years into your career, you have probably already forgotten some significant business-building milestones that could be the difference between winning the job and finishing second place. So, develop a list of all your achievements as if you were authoring a 10-page CV of your life's work and then determine which are most relevant to "humblebrag" and feature the next time you customize your resume or conduct an interview.

Bortz, D. (n.d.). *How To Humblebrag Your Way Into A New Job.* Monster. https://www.monster.com/career-advice/article/humble-brag-your-way-to-a-new-job-0217

PART II

Proceed Positively
On Your Journey

BE POSITIVE

*"Once you replace negative thoughts with positive ones,
you'll start having positive results."*

–Willie Nelson

You have every right to have a negative mindset. After all, you are out-of-work, and you may not have any solid job prospects on the immediate horizon. However, if you start from a place of negativity, it is also going to spread throughout your entire network. Instead, your positivity and a positive approach to your job search and prospecting will effectively rally others to mobilize and support your cause. "It is easy to dwell on the negative aspects of losing a job," commented a brand marketing veteran. "For the first six weeks after I was let go, it was hard for me to reconcile why I hadn't heard from certain people I worked with. I was as pleasantly surprised by the people I heard from as I was disappointed in the ones who hadn't reached out. Someone you might have said hello to and worked closely with for a period of time isn't necessarily your friend. Remember, it's business and it's transactional, so don't let it bother you or eat you up." When you exude a positive outlook, energy, and vibes, you inspire those who are in your network to go the extra mile on your behalf, and you motivate new contacts to join your network and your cause. Of course, there are going to be negative moments and experiences, but learn from them, shrug them off and proceed down the highway to positivity because it is that path that is going to deliver positive results and bring you closer to your next career opportunity.

PATIENCE, PERSISTENCE, AND POWER

"He that can have patience can have what he will."

–Ben Franklin

Patience, persistence, and power are all essential qualities for achieving success. Patience is the ability to wait for something without getting discouraged. It is important to be patient when you are working towards a goal because there will be times when things don't go your way. If you are patient, you will be more likely to stick with your goals and eventually achieve them. Persistence is the ability to keep trying even when things are difficult. It is important to be persistent when you are facing challenges because giving up is not an option. If you are persistent, you will be more likely to overcome the challenges and achieve your goals. Power is the ability to control your own destiny. It is important to have power when you are trying to achieve success because it will allow you to take control of your life and make things happen. If you have power, you will be more likely to achieve your goals and live the life you want.

Patience, persistence, and power are all within your reach. If you are willing to work hard and never give up, you can achieve anything you set your mind to. To navigate your path to success effectively, consider these guiding principles. Start by setting goals that are grounded in realism, ensuring they align with your capabilities and aspirations. Break these objectives down into manageable steps, making progress feel attainable. Remember to celebrate every triumph, regardless of its scale, to maintain motivation. Avoid the trap of comparing your journey to others, as each career path is unique. Lastly, cultivate a positive and unwavering focus on your objectives, and surround yourself with a supportive and uplifting circle of individuals who share your determination and optimism.

YOUR CAREER JOURNEY IS UNIQUE

"Your journey is completely yours. It is unique."

–Kemi Sogunle

While millions of people have experienced a transition in their professional career, whether forced or on their own terms, the first, and perhaps most important lesson, is that no two career transition journeys are the same. We touched on this important insight in the first section of this book. While we can learn extensive lessons and insights from those who have made a successful transition in their careers, each and every one of us takes our own unique journey based on our industry, past professional experience, education, members of our professional network, past clients, customers and colleagues, family, salary level, geographic location, life stage, money saved and invested, and future goals, objectives, dreams and ambitions. In other words, this is your one and only employment journey. The Minnesota State Colleges and Universities Careerwise digital hub summarized it well when they wrote, "Think of your career journey as climbing a ladder. Each step of the ladder could be a job that gives you a unique experience. At one job, you might pick up new skills. At another, you might gain a new interest. In all of your jobs, you'll collect valuable experiences." Because this is your unique career journey, you get to make the rules and navigate the ship. You get to determine how much sweat equity you want to invest or how many cup-of-coffee meetings you want to schedule. Most importantly, you get to author your own career transition playbook in the same way that NFL head coaches do before the game on Sunday. There is no right or wrong way to take your journey just like there is no right or wrong way to hike a mountain. There may be paths you will take that will prove to be more efficient, productive or easier to navigate, but that is part of the testing and learning you will do along your journey to the next destination in your professional career. Embrace and enjoy your unique career journey as it is the only one that will ever exist, and along the way, evolve and transform as you prepare to write the next chapter in your career.

Your Lifelong Journey. Minnesota State Careerwise. (n.d.). https://careerwise. minnstate.edu/careers/journey.html

CHANGE IS GREAT

*"You never change your life until you step out
of your comfort zone; change begins at the end
of your comfort zone."*

–Roy T. Bennett

Robin Sharma, one of the world's top leadership experts and author of *The Greatness Guide: 101 Lessons For Making What's Good At Work And Life Even Better*, said, "Change is hard at first, messy in the middle and gorgeous at the end." Simply translated, change is good. That change can be the transition from college to career, or from one job to the next. Perhaps there is no better way to describe a transition in your career and the changes it brings to you, your family, friends, and your way of living than Sharma's quote. However, once you battle through the hard part and muddle through the messy phase, your next act will be beautiful, fulfilling and rewarding. As we each get older and further along in our career, it is natural for all of us to settle into routines. From the time we wake up to the time we leave for work each day, our life becomes a series of regular routines. Routines feel comfortable and safe, but they also lull us to sleep so when a drastic change like a reduction in force or a forced retirement arrives at our workplace, it is "hard" as Sharma describes. Instead of fighting change, embrace it. Be transformative and innovative in your mindset and approach pursuing the next chapter in your career. Change will force you out of your routines and out of your comfort zone. That is a great thing. Change in your career will motivate you to reconnect with individuals in your network, dust off your resume and take inventory of your past, present and future. Change will also result in you meeting new people and making new connections. Change will challenge you strategically and creatively. Change will inspire you to learn and evolve so much more than if you kept your existing job and your existing routines for the next several years. Change is not only good. Change is great! Embrace change and be energized by it. Change will ultimately not only help you successfully make a career transition, but it will empower you to transform professionally and personally.

MOST PEOPLE ARE GIVERS

"When we give cheerfully and accept gratefully,
everyone is blessed."

–Maya Angelou

As you seek your next job, you must believe and be confident that the overwhelming majority of people in your professional and personal networks are "givers" and they want to help you on your journey. Some people have no interest in assisting your job seeking efforts any may not even respond to your email or LinkedIn message. Others may be talkers where they talk a big game, but don't actually deliver anything of substance to support your career transition. However, most people including your friends, family, former co-workers and college classmates are givers and want to make a measurable investment in helping you succeed in your job search. Even people you don't know yet, but who you will meet on your unique career journey, will want to "give" and help you. Adam Grant, an organizational psychologist who authored, *Give and Take: A Revolutionary Approach To Success*, agrees that most successful leaders are givers. In an interview with *Inc.*, he said,

"First, it's easier for leaders to multiply themselves and create networks of givers. To build cultures where that's the norm and, as a result, to be able to delegate a lot of the giving to people around and below them. That provides an opportunity to spread their giving farther than people who are not at the top." In his quote, Grant captures the essence of the network of giving that you need to immerse yourself in and leverage as you search for your next act. However, you need to arm all your givers, both leaders and those delegates who comprise their network of givers, with the right assets and ammunition to effectively assist you. Just because most people want to give does not mean they can do it on their own. They need the pieces to the puzzle that are going to make a connection to your next opportunity. In other words, you need to proactively communicate with them consistently and provide valuable information such as the job search tool we featured earlier in this book. If they are going to make an investment in giving to your career journey, you need to make an even greater investment in clearly identifying industries and organizations you are prospecting and the names of individuals you are trying to secure an audience with. In other words, make it as easy as possible for the "givers" to give.

Buchanan, L. (2013, April 5). *Why The Most Successful Leaders Are Givers*. Inc. https://www.inc.com/leigh-buchanan/adam-grant-leadership-give-and-take.html

PERFECT YOUR PUZZLE

"Each one of us fulfills a piece of a larger puzzle."

–Eric McCormack

Jo Green, a Career Change Coach, introduced the notion that transitioning in your career is like a jigsaw puzzle in a column she wrote titled, "Why Changing Your Career Is A Lot Like Doing A Jigsaw Puzzle." As she reminisced about her own career transition, Green wrote, "I recognized the need to see the small things come together, much like doing a big jigsaw puzzle. I needed to practice the twin arts of patience and pattern spotting. These are the same skills we use to piece together a jigsaw puzzle. Turning a mound of disconnected fragments into a satisfyingly complete and complex image takes time and tenacity. It also takes imagination and intuition. It's absorbing and frustrating and fun." If you can take this approach to the next opportunity in your career, it is like completing your own jigsaw puzzle. It will put you in the right mindset to manage, as Green describes, the frustrating and fun phases of your journey. Your puzzle pieces are the individuals in your network and those who you will meet along the way who will help you connect and complete your puzzle. The pieces are also a variety of puzzle-solving moments where you are inspired by others as well as the research you conduct, and right before your eyes, you will witness your puzzle starting to take shape. There will be frustrating days when you don't complete one piece of the puzzle and fun days when you complete entire sections. Either way, stay focused, positive, and confident in solving your puzzle because once you do, you will have successfully secured your next job opportunity.

Green, J. (2017, August 8). *Why Changing Your Career Is A Lot Like Doing A Jigsaw Puzzle.* Collective Hub. https://collectivehub.com/2017/08/why-changing-career-is-a-lot-like-doing-a-jigsaw-puzzle/

PURSUE YOUR PASSION

"Nothing is as important as passion.
No matter what you want to do with your life,
be passionate."

–Jon Bon Jovi

Billionaire Mark Cuban, owner of the NBA's Dallas Mavericks, proclaimed, "One of the great lies of life is 'follow your passions,'" as part of the Amazon Insights for Entrepreneurs series. Mr. Cuban, we respectfully disagree with you especially when it comes to an individual's career. There are many stories of individuals who not only successfully pursued their passion, but also converted their passion into a successful business as their second act. Perhaps, that passion did not translate into billions of dollars, but not everyone like you needs to earn a billion dollars to be successful and happy. Take Tom Waldron, a New Jersey State Trooper who retired at the age of 50 and then took his passion for fitness and exercise and transformed that passion into a personal training business that is now more than a decade into existence and can boast of hundreds if not thousands of happy clients. Tom could have sought and settled for a typical security job, but instead, he and his entrepreneurial spirit pursued his passion and the second act of his career led to him becoming the CEO of his own company, a company he was passionate about when he started it and is even more passionate about now more than a decade later. Tom commented, "I encourage anyone who is embarking on a second career to focus on an activity that they have a passion for and try to find a way to monetize it. The energy you bring to this new beginning will be off the charts which will maximize your chance for success." As you set off on your career transition journey, take quality time to map out all your passions – music, fashion, food, sports, education, travel, pets, classic cars, even fitness – and consider how you might convert that passion into your next act either as an employee of a company that specializes in that passion or, like Tom, the retired state police officer, as your own start-up company. There was never a law passed that regulated that you could not have fun at work. Instead, live by the famous quote, "Choose a job you love, and you will never have to work a day in your life." In order to accomplish that, your next act in your career must be one where you are applying your craft to something you are incredibly passionate about.

Clifford, C. (2018, February 9). *Billionaire Mark Cuban: "One Of The Great Lies Of Life Is Follow Your Passions."* CNBC. https://www.cnbc.com/2018/02/16/mark-cuban-follow-your-passion-is-bad-advice.html

IT WILL TAKE A VILLAGE

"I'm every woman. It takes a village to make me who I am."

–Katy Perry

Family, friends (old and new), neighbors, college classmates, professors, past colleagues, professional and personal contacts, the barista at your favorite coffee shop and the individuals who you play pickleball, golf or exercise with - each and every one could potentially play a role in helping you secure the next opportunity in your career. It will take a village to land your next job. In an article about the New Start Career Network in New Jersey, a journalist wrote that the organization, "is taking an innovative approach to ending unemployment by developing a village of volunteer coaches who are helping job seekers ages 45 and older, learn and apply practical job search techniques, and by offering hope and inspiration." Do not proceed one day thinking you will do it on your own. Put aside your pride and your ego. Equally important, keep your eyes and ears wide open each and every day throughout your transition. Perfect strangers may hold the key to unlocking the door to your next opportunity. The more proactive you are in your approach and the more time you invest in networking and scheduling meetings, not only will your village expand, but so will the number of opportunities. Ultimately, you will secure that next job, but it will most likely occur because of someone you knew who knew someone who knew someone who knew someone who knew someone who opened a door that you busted wide open! Earlier in this book, we featured setting SMART goals. One SMART goal that speaks to this lesson includes making one new meaningful professional connection each week. If you want to be more aggressive, make two new meaningful professional connections each week. Each of those new connections will open doors to new opportunities.

Schiavi, M. (2016, July 3). *Imagine: "It Takes A Village" To Help The Long-Term Unemployed.* My Central Jersey. https://www.mycentraljersey.com/story/money/business/2016/07/03/imagine-takes-village-help-long-term-unemployed/86569048/

ANYONE CAN OPEN THE DOOR TO YOUR NEXT OPPORTUNITY

"The best secret of success is to always be ready to find and open the door of opportunity."

–Debasish Mridha

In an article titled, "How To Convince Strangers To Help You Get A Job," Alex Lacey writes, "In my recent job search, I received referrals for 40 jobs at 40 hard-to-reach companies despite not knowing anyone at 38 of them." Lacey used strangers who he proactively introduced himself to on LinkedIn to help him secure his next job. As you transition, consistently keep an open mind with regard to meeting new people and the role they will potentially play in your journey.

"You never know where that job lead will come. I found my first corporate job out of college while waiting tables. A regular customer worked at a public relations firm and offered me a job solely based on the interactions we had at the restaurant," recalled a public relations veteran. Another executive commented, "Sometimes you just never really know who knows who. One of your friends or colleagues might have attended college with someone who can get you visibility with your next job destination of choice." When and where you least expect it, one meeting, one phone call, one email or one chance encounter with a total stranger could be the connection to your next opportunity. Each day when you wake, set out on your day with the objective to meet and network with as many new people as possible. Each person you meet will help you complete the jigsaw puzzle that is your journey to the next opportunity in your career.

Lacey, A. (2017, December 31). *How To Convince Strangers To Help You Get A Job*. Free Code Camp. https://www.freecodecamp.org/news/how-to-convince-strangers-to-help-you-get-a-job-35db34549ac4/

SUCCESS IS A MARATHON

"Success is a marathon of consistency,
walked out one day at a time."

–Billy Alsbrooks

While most individuals who find themselves searching for their next job, come out of the blocks like a sprinter thinking they will be back at work in the next month or two, it is better to start your journey with the mindset and mental toughness of a marathoner because you are most likely in the running for a longer race than you expected and along the way, just like a marathoner, you are going to need to slow down to refuel and pace yourself so that you can successfully reach the finish line. A senior marketing communications executive commented, "Preparing yourself for a longer journey will help minimize the emotional valleys when disappointments come along. You're in it for the long haul and your mind should reflect that." In an article titled, "The Job Search is a Marathon, not a Sprint – Treat it as such," the reporter writes, "All too often, a day feels like a week and a week can feel like a month – particularly for those who haven't had to look for a job in years." Your marathon is going to consist of thousands of phone calls, texts and emails with the allies in your network. It's also going to feature the submission and completion of many applications as well as a series of informal and formal interviews via Zoom, phone, one-on-one, panels and even committees. If it was easy, everyone who is out of work would be right back at a new job. However, it is not easy. It is painful - physically, mentally and emotionally. It can play tricks with your mind and psyche like miles 20 through 26 in a marathon. Mark Beal, one of the co-authors of this book, knows this well as he has successfully completed five marathons including the iconic Boston Marathon. If you can start and continue your journey with the mindset that you are going to run a marathon for the next six to 12 months and each day is another mile on your journey, your unique finish line will come into focus on your own time based on the path you have taken. As many marathoners will tell you, "Enjoy your journey to the finish line." In this case, your finish line is successfully securing your next job. Along this journey to that successful destination, enjoy each cup-of- coffee meeting, informational interview, reconnection with a former colleague and moment of learning and inspiration.

The Job Search Is A Marathon, Not A Sprint - Treat It As Such. Career Attraction. (n.d.). https://careerattraction.com/marathon/

SWALLOW YOUR PRIDE

*"Please swallow your pride. If I have things
you need to borrow. For no one can fill those
of your needs that you won't let show."*

–Bill Withers.

There is no room for pride when you are searching for the next job in your career, especially if your job search is the result of an unexpected transition such as a layoff or a reduction in force. In other words, don't be so proud that you are afraid to share the news that you were laid off or your company had a reduction in force. One executive in a career transition said, "As a public relations and marketing communications professional, it might seem odd that I had a hard time with this during my transition. And that probably was a mistake. My reasons were numerous, including being unsure of exactly what I wanted to do next, which made it more difficult to clearly and succinctly share with people in my network what I was after. And if that is the case with you, then I would recommend having the confidence to share that your answer could be different to different people depending upon the role you are seeking and the type of industry job you are chasing." Don't be so proud that you don't ask for help, support and assistance from those allies in your network. Don't be so proud that you won't attend a career support networking group meeting. Don't be so proud that you don't share thought leadership or content about your unique career transition on your social and professional channels. Don't be so proud that you don't seek out and schedule informal cup-of-coffee meetings to ask questions and learn. Don't be so proud that you don't mobilize your contacts when you formally apply for a job. Don't be so proud that you don't learn from rejection. In an article titled, "5 Reasons You Should Swallow Your Pride and Ask for Feedback After Getting Rejected," Kat Boogaard writes, "Getting rejected is never fun. And, asking for input and advice afterward can undoubtedly be a little awkward. But that doesn't change the fact that it's the perfect opportunity to gain some useful insight into ways you can better yourself— and your job hunt! So, swallow your pride and hit 'reply' on that dreaded rejection email." No matter the circumstances that have you seeking your next career opportunity, put your pride aside during the transition and pick it up again when you secure that new job and you are back to work.

Boogaard, K. (2020, June 19). *5 Reasons You Should Swallow Your Pride And Ask For Feedback After Getting Rejected*. The Muse. https://www.the muse.com/advice/5-reasons-you-should-swallow-your-pride-and-ask-for-feedback-after-getting-rejected

OWN YOUR JOURNEY

*"All people got dreams. Don't be afraid to get up
on your feet. Don't be afraid to live what you believe."*

–Tom Petty

"We aspire to a higher level of human achievement. The power to create and become who we want is in our minds and in our hands. We design our journey and the life we are called to live." Christopher Connors penned those inspiring words in a column he wrote about the journey to a job titled, "You Design Your Journey – Not Your Job." As discussed earlier in this book, you are the owner, operator, CEO and CMO of your journey to your next career opportunity so own every aspect of it. As you transition, own the setbacks. If you look to others to take ownership, you are giving up control of your journey. Yes, you will have an army of allies who will be eager to lend their assistance and support, but you need to own every one of those relationships and every step and meeting that you take with them. You are the only one who can take ownership of your unique journey each and every day. As the CEO and CMO of your one and only career journey, you will have deputies and partners, but you will need to own the go-to-market campaign and set the strategy as well as the activation tactics.

Connors, C. D. (2017, November 8). *You Design Your Journey - Not Jour Job*. Medium. https://chrisdconnors.medium.com/you-design-your-journey-not-your-job-89a26ded8ca8

ENJOY YOUR JOURNEY

"Enjoy the journey and try to get better every day. And don't lose the passion and the love for what you do."

–Nadia Comaneci

As you immerse yourself in the professional networking and job search process, enjoy each and every moment. When you get the opportunity to participate in informational interviews, embrace them. When you get a call back for a second interview, celebrate it. When you conduct research in advance of an interview, attack it with exuberance. Along your journey to your next career position, enjoy reuniting with classmates and catching up with former colleagues. Be inspired by the lightbulb moments on your journey. There will be many of them. In other words, don't commiserate the many steps along the way. Instead, enjoy them. A positive and optimistic approach can transform your search for your next job into a great adventure instead of series of arduous tasks. Having a positive mindset and enjoying each step of the journey is something that is so contagious it will catch the attention of potential employers and engage them. That type of mindset is exactly what they are looking to add to their organization and culture.

THERE WILL BE GOOD DAYS & BAD DAYS

"You have to remember that the hard days are what make you stronger. The bad days make you realize what a good day is. If you never had any bad days, you would never have that sense of accomplishment."

–Aly Raisman

"Job searching is hard. It's hard for most people – for me, for you, for your friend's cousin," wrote Alyse Kalish in an article titled, "How To Pull Yourself Through A Rough Job Search When You Feel Like Giving Up." Until that day when you win the recruiting and selection process and are offered a formal employment contract, you will most likely have more bad days than good days on your way to the next opportunity in your career. Every job rejection or remark that you are overqualified or last-minute cancellation of an important networking meeting will contribute to a negative attitude and mindset. "There will be very dark days that will lead you to question yourself, regardless of the reason for leaving your previous job," said Keith Green, a marketing and public relations practitioner. "You will go on an emotional roller coaster picturing yourself in new and potentially exciting roles as opportunities arise. And if you are looking at jobs that would require you to move, the mental part of that is also difficult. The level of uncertainty can get you down, but fight through it because something better is coming next." Learn lessons from the setbacks and failures and quickly proceed ahead on a positive path. You want to start to recall all the small victories that you have had on your journey that put you in a position for an opportunity to be a finalist or that helped you secure an audience with key decision makers. Positivity is contagious and infectious. By being positive in everything you do - posting content, participating in career networking meetings and proactively networking - you will engage and mobilize your followers in a way that will create a positive movement on your behalf that will lead to the ultimate victory, the next opportunity in your career.

Kalish, A. (2020, June 19). *How To Pull Yourself Through A Rough Job Search When You Feel Like Giving Up*. The Muse. https://www.themuse.com/advice/how-to-pull-yourself-through-a-rough-job-search-when-you-feel-like-giving-up

STAY THE COURSE

"Whatever course you decide upon, there is always someone to tell you that you are wrong. There are always difficulties arising which tempt you to believe that your critics are right. To map out a course of action and follow it to an end requires courage."

–Ralph Waldo Emerson

In 2024 and beyond on your unique journey to your next career opportunity, there are going to be many starts, stops and even detours. There will probably even be a few exit ramps. No matter what, stay the course. In other words, as you take your unique career journey and learn from the wins and the losses, as well as the advice and counsel from a wide variety of individuals and sources, including the critics and naysayers, continue to stay the course towards your ultimate objective – securing that new job opportunity that you have been strategically targeting and prospecting. A senior marketer said, "Whenever possible, stay clear of naysayers. If someone says, 'who are you to think you can achieve success.' Remind them 'who am I to think that I can't.'" Surround yourself with positive allies and collaborators. Eliminate the naysayers and anyone who is exuding negative vibes from your village of supporters. You must continuously remind yourself that this is your unique career journey. You are the map maker and the navigator. You will have first mates and second mates along the way, but as the captain, it is all up to you to stay the course to your ultimate destination and do that with the crew that is rowing with you, not against you.

SURROUND YOURSELF WITH SUPPORTERS

"Surround yourself with only people who are going to lift you higher."

–Oprah Winfrey

World traveler, adventurer and author Leon Logothetis wrote, "When you're surrounded by good people, you're surrounded by life. You'll be less stressed and find more joy in daily things. Today, make a commitment to start spending more time with the good people in your life." Leon was writing about surrounding yourself with good people and supporters in life, not your job search, but the same principle applies to your career. There is no room on your journey for negativity. There is no room for people on the ship you are captaining who use the word, "can't" in their vocabulary. As you embark on your unique career journey, you are going to quickly learn which individuals in your personal and professional network are going to rally to support your cause and those who are just giving you lip service and don't have enough concern or interest to invest their time or effort. "My wife was tremendous during my transition. She knew exactly when I needed support and to talk, and when to give me my space. There's a bit of an art form to that, and she was incredibly helpful through the highs and lows," commented Keith Green, a marketing and communications professional. Align yourself with all of those individuals who show genuine support and will deliver value in the form of assistance. When it comes to your supporters, it will be a case of quality over quantity. Ten quality supporters will deliver greater value, counsel and positive mojo to you than 100 acquaintances. Surround yourself each and every day with your true supporters – individuals who are consistently positive in their mindset, attitude and support.

Logothetis, L. (2015, March 6). *Keeping Good Company: Why You Should Surround Yourself With Good People.* Huff Post. https://www.huffpost. com/entry/kkeeping-good-company-why-you-should-surround- yourself-with-good-people_b_6816468

FIND YOUR TRIBE

*"Surround yourself with good people.
People who are going to be honest with you
and look out for your best interest."*

–Derek Jeter

You are who you choose to hang around with. Simply put, if you want to be successful, you will position yourself in an environment where people are constantly achieving success. If you want to be a CEO, you have to be around CEOs and leaders of organizations. That can also include the 4.0 GPA student group, teammates who always have incredible highlights and stats, and even those who thrive under an immense amount of pressure to meet and exceed expectations. Your tribe will have a profound effect on who you are and will become. A tribe is a group of people who are connected by a common interest, goal, or belief. Guy Winch Ph.D. provided a very strong perspective of a tribe stating, "Today, our "tribe" is often our immediate family—those with whom we live and share meals. However, given the fractured nature of today's families (picture five people sitting in different rooms, each absorbed with their own screen), and given that unmarried adults often live alone or with roommates, our "need to belong" often goes partially or substantially unmet." We live in a multicultural world where so many paths are crossed along the way to success, and choosing your tribe is a great strategy for achieving success.

Tribes can be a powerful force for good. They can provide support, encouragement, and motivation to help you reach your goals. They can also provide you with a sense of belonging and community. Here are some specific ways that a tribe can help you reach your goals and achieve personal and professional success:

- Support: Your tribe can provide you with support when you are feeling discouraged or lost. They can offer you encouragement and advice to help you stay on track.

- Motivation: Your tribe can motivate you to keep going when things get tough. They can remind you of your goals and why you are working so hard to achieve them.

- Learning: Your tribe can be a source of knowledge and learning. They can share their experiences and expertise to help you grow and develop.

- Connection: Your tribe can provide you with a sense of connection and community. They can make you feel like you are not alone.

- Creativity: Your tribe can help you tap into your creativity. They can offer you new ideas and perspectives to help you solve problems and come up with new solutions.

- Recognition: Your tribe can recognize your achievements and help you celebrate your successes. This can boost your confidence and motivation to keep going.

If you are looking to reach your goals and achieve personal and professional success, finding your tribe is essential. Surround yourself with people who believe in you and who will support you along the way. There is an African proverb that goes, "If you want to fast, go alone. If you want to go far, go together." Finding your tribe comes down to the life you want to live, and only you can determine the speed and distance. These tips are helpful in finding your tribe:

- Start by identifying your interests and goals: What are you passionate about? What do you want to achieve? Once you know what you are looking for, you can start to find people who share your interests and goals.

- Join online communities or groups: There are many online communities and groups where you can connect with people who share your interests. This is a great way to meet new people and start building relationships.

- Attend events or workshops: Another way to meet new people is to attend events or workshops related to your interests. This is a great way to meet people in person and learn from them.

- Be open to new experiences: Don't be afraid to step outside of your comfort zone and meet new people. The more people you meet, the more likely you are to find your tribe.

Finding your tribe takes time and effort, but it is worth it. You have a long career ahead of you and an even longer life to live. Surround yourself with people who believe in you and who will support you along the way. You will be amazed at how much you can achieve.

Winch, G. (2020, February 19). *The Importance Of Belonging To A Tribe.* Psychology Today. https://www.psychologytoday.com/us/blog/the-squeaky-wheel/202002/the-importance-belonging-tribe

PERSEVERANCE CREATES OPPORTUNITIES

"Success is no accident. It is hard work, perseverance, learning, studying, sacrifice and most of all, love of what you are doing or learning to do."

–Pele

A November 13, 2022 article in *Forbes* authored by Tracy Brower shares, "New data suggests finding your next job may be tougher than it was even a few months ago. But you can persevere and find your best fit role – if you understand how to shore up your strategies to get through."

By definition, according to Webster's Dictionary, perseverance means the continued effort to do or achieve something despite difficulties, failure, or opposition. If that doesn't sound like searching for a job in the midst of a career transition, nothing does. Each and every day of your job search, there will be hurdles, roadblocks, rejection and failure. You have two choices. You could give in to the setbacks and determine that you will never work again. However, we all know that is not true. So, instead of delaying the inevitable of securing that next job opportunity, push through the obstacles immediately and demonstrate a high degree of perseverance and persistence. If you can demonstrate these admirable qualities, it will positively mobilize your personal and professional network while helping you secure your next opportunity sooner.

Brower, T. (2022, November 13). *Finding A Job Is Tougher Now: 5 Practical Tips To Persevere.* Forbes. https://www.forbes.com/sites/tracybrower/2022/11/13/finding-a-job-is-tougher-now-5-practical-tips-to-persevere/?sh=361c6da631d5

CREATE YOUR OWN DESTINY

*"It is not in the stars to hold our destiny
but in ourselves."*

–William Shakespeare

In a column titled, "7 Tips For Creating Your Own Destiny," Kevin Daum writes, "Too many people whine about not having the life they want. The main reason people fall short of their own expectations is the same reason most companies fail to achieve their objectives: poor planning and execution." Throughout this book, we have emphasized that the career journey that you are traveling on is your own unique journey. Well, the same can be said about creating your own destiny. There are no rules regulating how you go about creating your next job opportunity. We highlight that in the first few lessons of this book. It's one of the reasons we wrote this book so that you could apply as many or as few of these lessons to your unique journey so that you could create your own destiny. You should seek guidance, counsel, recommendations, tips and lessons like those featured in this book, but you and you alone will create your own destiny and your own path to your future job and career. Today, you may have no idea where that destiny will take you, but everything you invest – research, referrals and reunions with former colleagues and classmates – will empower you to create your own destiny. A destiny that you will turn around and share with others in need once you have secured your next opportunity.

Daum, K. (2012, August 17). *7 Tips For Creating Your Own Destiny*. Inc. https://www.inc.com/kevin-daum/7-tips-for-creating-your-own-destiny.html

LEARNING IS A JOURNEY

"The more that you read, the more things you will know.
The more that you learn, the more places you'll go."

–Dr. Seuss

It's only after we graduate college, and we begin our careers, that the real learning begins. For many years, you have learned on the job. Well now, you are going to learn so much more off the job. You are going to learn more about human relations than even before. You are going to learn about what motivates individuals in your network to act on your behalf. You are going to learn how challenging it is to strategically navigate your way into a corner office meeting at one of the organizations you have been targeting and prospecting. Embrace and celebrate everything you are learning. Consider this search for your next job, the greatest final exam you will ever take in your life, but you already know you are going to earn an "A" because one day, all your preparation and studying and learning is going to pay off. Learning is a journey, and your career journey will take you to your ultimate destination but take time each day to enjoy each step of your journey and the learnings along the way.

LEARN FROM YOUR LOSSES

*"You learn more from losing than winning.
You learn to keep going."*

–Morgan Wootten

Henry Ford stated, "Failure is simply the opportunity to begin again, this time more intelligently." In your career, you are going to experience failure at least once or you will never be in a transitional phase. The most important thing you can do is to learn from each failure and approach the next opportunity as intelligently as Ford emphasizes. Each time you interview for a job and don't get it, ask for the reasons why. Whether you were eliminated from contention after your first interview or advanced all the way to the final round, ask the recruiter for specific reasons why someone was selected over you. Typically, you will receive a response like, "It was a very difficult decision and you finished a very close second." As Ricky Bobby states in *Talladega Nights*, "If you ain't first, you're last." While they may be trying to be kind in giving you that type of response, that doesn't help you at all. Instead ask by saying, "As I interview for other jobs, I would love to learn from this process. Can you provide me some constructive criticism that I can learn from and apply to my next opportunity?" In exchange for the investment in time and resources that you made for a job application and interview process that could have taken weeks if not months, you have to take away key lessons and learnings and immediately apply those to the next opportunity. There is no greater waste of time and effort than not learning valuable lessons from the losses and failures including not winning the job that you invested many hours in applying, researching, preparing, and interviewing for. Your investment of time and effort in not securing the job you pursued must be rewarded with insightful lessons and learnings that you can apply to the next job opportunity that you are proactively prospecting.

EXPERIENCE IS EARNED

"Experience is one thing you can't get for nothing."

–Oscar Wilde

Yoga teacher and author Stephanie Spence said, "Experience is earned, not randomly gained. Wisdom is given to those who work for it. If it was easy to grow everyone would do it." Stephanie's "Experience is earned," quote is as applicable to your career journey as any other quote. As you advance on your unique career journey, you will be earning valuable experience with every meeting, interview and proactive participation in a career networking support group or industry meet-up. With those experiences will come wisdom that should fuel your next set of strategic moves. You are not only working to earn that wisdom, but you are also working to apply it to the individuals and companies you are targeting and prospecting. As Spence concludes, "If it was easy to grow, everyone would do it." Celebrate that you are growing each and every day. Celebrate the experienced earned, the wisdom gained, and your growth and transformation is leading you in a positive direction to the next opportunity in your career. Each and every day of your job search, you are experiencing a transformation that is contributing to your personal and professional evolution.

DON'T FORGET KARMA

"When you truly understand karma, then you realize you are responsible for everything in your life."

–Keanu Reeves

Whether you call it destiny or fate, just like the "favor bank" we feature later in this book, positive karma can always come back in your favor when you least expect it, or you need it the most. Each and every day, continue to share positive energy and vibes and your network will rally around that positivity. Even as you seek help, continue to assist others in need. While your greatest priority will be to secure your next career opportunity, someone in your network may call you out of the blue to help their son or daughter get an internship with a company you have a relationship with. Yes, it will take you a few minutes away from your focus, but your investment in time and resources to help someone else will only help you somewhere down the road. That's why you never forget karma, especially positive karma. In a February 15, 2022 post, Tony Beshara titled her thought leadership, "Karma Will Help You Get A Job." Tony writes, "I saw that the successful job seekers shared common characteristics, and that they were taking certain actions that made the job search easier for them... In other words, you have to escape your self-centered focus and pained emotions and concentrate on what you can do for others."

Beshara, T. (n.d.). *Tip #28 Karma Will Help You Get A Job*. Tony Beshara. https://www.tonybeshara.com/tip-28-karma-will-help-you-get-a-job/

LEAVE THE PAST BEHIND & CREATE A FUTURE VISION

*"Once you make the decision to move on,
don't look back. Your destiny will never be found
in the rear-view mirror."*

–Mandy Hale

Your LinkedIn profile and resume are not your life's biography or obituary. Your career journey is not about where you've been. It's about where you are going and what you want to do. Flip the bit and think of this from the employer's point-of-view. The work environment and the needs of employers are changing rapidly in 2024 and beyond due to the digital revolution. Employers need employees with strong competencies to help their firm meet this challenge. Therefore, jettison those things that are painting you as a "legacy" resource and identify those things that are consistent with presenting you as a candidate that you have the skills and competencies that they need to fulfill their strategic goals and achieve success. As you go through your resume and LinkedIn profile ensure that you carefully select PARs (Problem Action Result, you will see this featured in future lessons) and word them in such a way that they convey an image of you that matches the employer's needs - never put anything false down, but always write within the constraints of your actual experience and capabilities. You need to do the same thing on your LinkedIn profile by carefully selecting those skills that are in high demand that you possess. This also applies to your professional references so that they include verbiage in their recommendation that highlights your skills and experience consistent with the opportunities you are pursuing.

MASTER THE SIX DEGREES OF YOUR JOB SEARCH

"Six degrees of separation doesn't mean that everyone is linked to everyone else in just six steps. It means that a very small number of people are linked to everyone else in a few steps, and the rest of us are linked to the world through those special few."

–Malcolm Gladwell

The world we live in is all driven by six degrees of separation. Think of the popular "Six Degree of Kevin Bacon." We are all connected. In your job search, it is all about maximizing and leveraging those connections to deliver success. So, grow and nurture your contacts and your network so that you evolve them into relationships that you can tap into to maximize the benefit that your network can deliver for you. "Cultivate your contacts by offering them something of value, when they don't expect it," says Paul Capelli, whose 30-year career includes communication leadership positions at Fortune 500 companies, leading media organizations and top-ranked agencies. "It need be only a simple bit of information or thought that shows you are thinking of others best interests -- everyone likes a heads-up on a new idea; an emerging trend; a new source of information online, etc." Focus and set a specific time each week that you invest in growing your contacts and strengthening the relationships with those in your network both during the job search, at the firm where you land your next job, and throughout your career once you are back working. So many individuals succumb to the pitfall that they don't have the time to continue networking proactively, but with digital disruption impacting businesses, many workers are finding themselves in transition more than once in their career. Therefore, it is critical to stay connected and continuously be working to grow and strengthen your network. Your success will be helped greatly by making the six degrees of separation work for you. Capelli adds, "When the time comes, it's much easier to ask of your network for a referral, job lead or recommendation, knowing you have established yourself as a 'giver' not just a connection that reaches out in times of need."

PART III

Take Proactive Action To Drive Measurable Results

BE PROACTIVE

*"Everyone must be proactive and do all they can
to help themselves to stay employed."*

–Stephen Covey

In a column titled, "5 Ways To Stop Feeling Helpless and Start Taking the Job Hunt Into Your Own Hands," Lily Zhang writes, "One thing that's important to acknowledge is how critical it is to stay motivated. Sending in your materials to one job and then waiting around with fingers crossed won't do that for you. You need to stay driven in order to keep the ball in your court." If you take only one lesson away from this book, this is the one, be proactive in everything you do throughout your career transition. A reactive or passive approach to prospecting for your next job opportunity will get you nowhere. From setting your alarm in the morning to getting a jumpstart on the day's agenda to making a conscious effort each day to expand your network, don't sit around waiting for the phone to ring or for an organization to respond to a resume you submitted. There will be times when you need to be reactive when opportunity knocks, but the only way opportunity is ever going to knock is as a result of your consistent proactive mindset, approach and execution. Stephen Covey said it best. "People who end up with the good jobs are the proactive ones who are solutions to problems, not problems themselves, who seize the initiative to do whatever is necessary to get the job done."

Zhang, L. (2020, June 19). *5 Ways To Stop Feeling Helpless And Start Taking The Job Hunt Into Your Own Hands*. The Muse. https://www.themuse.com/advice/5-ways-to-stop-feeling-helpless-and-start-taking-the-job-hunt-into-your-own-hands

REV UP YOUR MORNING ROUTINE

"Wake up early and tackle the day before it tackles you."

–Evan Carmichael

"Early to bed and early to rise makes a man healthy, wealthy and wise." Ben Franklin is credited with uttering this famous phrase more than 225 years ago, but it is more relevant today than ever for anyone who is in the midst of a job search. More recently in an August 2, 2023 article, *Fast Company* featured the Gen Z movement #5to9before9to5. The article reports, "The latest TikTok trend, '5 to 9 before 9 to 5,' has twentysomethings waking bright and early in an effort to reclaim their time. They're routinely waking up at 4:30 a.m. or even earlier so they can exercise, meditate, or basically just do whatever they want before the workday begins. While it sounds fairly exhausting, many report feeling energized, happier, and more accomplished." While it is very important to use a transition in your career as a time to break out and disrupt the regular routines that you got used to while you were in your last job, that doesn't mean that you should be sleeping in until 12:00 noon. The one routine that you should maintain... or

115

actually rev up, is setting your alarm clock and waking up early to take on the challenges of the day. If your former routine included rising early and exercising before commuting to your job, continue to do so and wake up even earlier. Getting off to a strong, confident and energizing start each day will provide you positive momentum as you proactively prospect your target companies while reacting to any unexpected opportunities that arrive via phone, email or a LinkedIn message. If you even want to take it one step further, dress for success, and get out of your pajamas and into a suit and tie or at least business casual attire. Whatever helps you best jumpstart each day of your unique journey, just do it. Nobody else is going to do it for you.

Bregel, S. (2023, August 2). *5 To 9 Before 9 To 5: Early Risers On TikTok Are Dispelling The Myth That Gen Z Is Lazy*. Fast Company. https://www.fast company.com/90932340/5-to-9-before-9-to-5-trend-tiktok-gen-z-workers-early?utm_source=briefing&utm_medium=email&utm_campaign=brands_am&utm_content=080323

DO SOMETHING
FOR THE FIRST TIME

*"What would life be if we had no courage
to attempt anything."*

–Vincent Van Gogh

A sk yourself, "When was the last time you did something for the first time?" That question was popular well before Darius Rucker led off his 2017 hit song, "For The First Time," with that question. It is human nature for individuals to get comfortable in their routines as they approach their 30s, 40s, 50s and 60s. Think back to when you were a teenager and all your "firsts" – first job, first paycheck, first car, first time driving, first time moving away from home. All of those "firsts" were about exploring and discovering new people, places and experiences. That is exactly what you need to do now. You need to recapture your teenage zest (or today's Gen Z zest) for discovery and exploration. This is the time to break your routines. Similar to today's workplace where traditional routines have been broken since the arrival of the pandemic in

2020, take that bold step and do something for the first time - attend your first career networking support group meeting, message someone who you don't know on LinkedIn, attempt to make a meaningful connect with a recruiter at a company that you have identified as one of your top places to work. For the first time, meet one-on-one with a career coach and determine if they can be of assistance. For the first time, ask your former colleagues for assistance and support. You may be hesitant, but the vast majority of them want to help you. They just need your direction. At least once a week throughout your career transition, you should be "doing something for the first time" – and enjoying every minute of it. We can promise you that doing something for the first time as it relates to your career will transform you and your job search.

PUT YOURSELF OUT THERE

"It's very hard to put yourself out there, it's very hard to be vulnerable, but those people who do that are the dreamers, the thinkers and the creators. They are the magic people of the world."

–Amy Poehler

In a blog post titled, "Putting Yourself Out There: Taking Steps To Land A Job," Danielle Dresden writes, "Getting noticed is the key to getting work of any kind. And these days, with fewer jobs and more ways to promote yourself, simply answering ads and sending in resumes is a sure way to get stuck on the sidelines." No matter the reason that you are in a transition in your career, now is the time to be proactive and vocal even if that has not been your style. As Dresden notes, you need to be an active participant in the career transition game and simply submitting your resume to online job postings is considered standing on the sidelines in today's social and digital media society. Meetups, career networking meetings, mix and mingles – no matter what they call it, if it involves people coming together to network and discuss jobs and careers, you need to attend and be a proactive participant. It also means scheduling one-on-one cup-of-coffee meetings and shaking as many hands as you are able like you are running for office. Whether it is former college classmates, past work colleagues or strangers who you meet at a career transition networking meeting, every person you meet can help you complete the jigsaw puzzle that is your transition to your next job opportunity. While for many of us, "putting yourself out there" is uncomfortable and maybe even feel a bit weird, it is a necessary step in your career transition journey. Yes, you can put yourself out there by blogging and tweeting, but you also need to do it the old school way by meeting people face-to-face, sharing your brand narrative and asking for assistance. So, start scheduling one-on-one meetings with as many people in your network as you are able to and conduct a simple online search for any meetups in your region whether they are career transition meetings or gatherings that are specifically focused on the industry where you are pursuing your next opportunity. Each meeting you schedule, or attend will empower you by expanding your network and learning new insights and information that will inform and inspire your next series of moves to that next opportunity.

Dresden, D. Putting Yourself Out There: Taking Steps To Land A Job. https://workbloom.com/job-search/putting-yourself-out-there-taking-steps-to-land-a-job.aspx

DUST OFF YOUR ROLODEX

*"Networking is not about just connecting people.
It's about connecting people with people,
people with ideas, and people with opportunities."*

–Michele Jennae

For those who are old enough to know what a Rolodex is, you should easily understand what this lesson means. For those who are not of age including members of Gen Z, this lesson could simply be called, "Review Your LinkedIn Contacts," or "Scroll Through Your Contacts On Your Phone." You have probably accrued more contacts then you will ever remember, but once a contact, always a contact. The easiest way to manage this process is to simply review all your contacts on LinkedIn alphabetically. Of course, there will be some contacts who you never really had much contact with at all. But, like finding a needle in a haystack, you will start to come across names of people who you collaborated closely with at one time but have just not stayed in contact with. Many of those individuals have gone on to new organizations in senior roles where they most likely can provide assistance especially if you are both still in the same industry. On September 24, 2022, *The New York Times* published an article featuring a five-year social experiment conducted by LinkedIn with 20 million users. The sub headline of the article claims, "A study that looked back at those tests found that relatively weak social connections were more helpful in finding jobs than stronger social ties." PJ Brovak, a leader in marketing communications echoed this sentiment. "What I found so humbling to me during my search process was that people who I hadn't worked directly with in more than 15 years were so willing to make introductions and recommend me to those in their networks." There is no room for an ego when you are going through a career transition, so put your ego and everything else aside and catch-up with former colleagues and past contacts and learn what doors they may be able to open. The worst thing that could happen is that they don't return your LinkedIn message or your phone call. If that is the case, they probably weren't going to deliver much value to your journey to your next career opportunity.

Singer, N. (2022, September 24). *LinkedIn Ran Social Experiments On 20 Million Users Over Five Years*. The New York Times. https://www.nytimes.com/2022/09/24/business/linkedin-social-experiments.html

RECONNECT WITH FORMER CONTACTS

*"We want to renew our vows with our people.
We want to reconnect with our people. We want
to get our people excited again."*

–Cyril Ramaphosa

Former classmates, professors, co-workers, colleagues, neighbors, fellow members of associations and groups that you belonged to are a great way to build, grow and mobilize your network. In this book, we write about how you can take your email contact list and LinkedIn has an automated way of comparing these contacts identifying matches and automatically requesting that they connect with you on LinkedIn. Going to expos, joining networking groups, attending professional association meetings is a great way to identify potential contacts but it is up to you to put in the effort to establish relationships with these contacts and then maintain those relationships. "A similar tactic is to reconnect with your university. Almost every school will have a career exploration center for students and alums, so take advantage and see what jobs and resources your alma mater has available," commented Keith Green, a longtime marketer who has also taught at several universities. So, plan time both when employed and when not, to focus on growing your contacts, nurturing your relationships, and making your network as strong as you are able. Keith Ferrazzi authored the book, *Who's Got Your Back*, and speaks to how to effectively work with your contacts to ensure you create and nurture strong relationships with those in your network.

CREATE CONNECTIONS WITH CUP-OF-COFFEE MEETINGS

*"I force people to have coffee with me, just because
I don't trust that a friendship can be maintained
without any other senses besides a computer
or cellphone screen."*

–John Cusack

There is no less intimidating way to secure a meeting with someone you are targeting and prospecting than simply asking if they would like to meet over a cup-of-coffee. In a column that one of the authors of this book, Mark Beal, wrote for *Grit Daily*, titled, "Hey Gen Z: Good Ol' Human Interaction Is Still Core To Landing Those Entry Level Jobs," Beal writes, "Almost every executive at one of your target companies will take a cup-of-coffee meeting because there's no risk and most people want to give back and help... (those) attempting to break into the business. But for you, the cup-of-coffee meeting is critically important and offers a low risk, high reward opportunity. First, a cup-of-coffee meeting gets you into the building. It gives you an opportunity to see inside your target company. If you execute your cup-of-coffee meeting at a high level, it will allow you to bypass the robotic and tech-centric recruitment process...and enables you to establish a powerful ally on the inside who could get your resume in front of the right recruiter." Forget the steak dinners and two-martini lunches, all it takes is a simple cup-of-coffee to successfully create a connection with someone who can be converted into your advocate as you strategically target a role at an organization where they may have influence. In today's world, that can even be a virtual cup-of-coffee meeting over Zoom, Microsoft Teams, or any other virtual platforms. Make it as easy as possible for the individual who you are prospecting with. Make it so easy that they can't refuse. Use cup-of-coffee meetings to your advantage as they do not come with the stress and anxiety of formal interviews. Instead, use them to listen and conduct research while simultaneously making a positive impression with a new member of your professional network. Your objective is simple – by the time you both complete drinking your coffee, you will want to impress the person on the other side of the table enough that they are motivated to act on your behalf and make calls and connections for you, ultimately helping you complete your one-of-a-kind career jigsaw puzzle. Keith Green, a veteran marketing executive added, "Don't be afraid to use this tactic in reverse, either. I've lost count of how many cups-of-coffee I have had over the years with people who were looking for a job and wanted to network. That said, many of those same people you made time for might be in a position to help you now in your career. So, seek those people out and ask them to meet for coffee." A decade ago, Megan Gebhart authored *52 Cups of Coffee*. The book's description reinforces this lesson. "When Megan Gebhart graduated college in 2011, she knew she couldn't resign herself to life at an aimless 9-to-5 job climbing the corporate ladder. So instead, she challenged herself to have a single cup of coffee with a different person every week for a year to see what lessons she could learn about life and careers." As you seek your next job, schedule your weekly cup-of-coffee, and explore where it may take your career. As highlighted earlier in this book, securing a weekly cup-of-coffee meeting can serve as on one of your metrics for success as you seek your next career opportunity.

Beal, M. (2019, March 10). *Hey Gen Z: Good 'Ol Human Interaction Is Still Core To Landing Those Entry Level Jobs*. Grit Daily. https://gritdaily.com/job-search/

BE PROFESSIONAL, PERSISTENT & PROACTIVE IN YOUR FOLLOW-UP

"The only guarantee for failure is to stop trying."

–John C. Maxwell

While securing informational interviews and professional networking meetings are important, the follow-up is even more critical. Too often, candidates circle back after an interview or a meeting and ask how they should follow-up because they have not heard anything. They need to be proactive and persistent in their follow-up. The onus is not on the interviewer to follow-up. That is the candidate's responsibility. For every interview you conduct, you should have a strategic timeline to guide your follow-up. After writing and sending a thank you note as highlighted in a lesson in this book, you should send a smart email the next week. A smart email could reference a news story that is relevant to your conversation. You should continue your follow-up every few weeks to maintain contact and provide updates. If the interview was regarding a position, then you will want to be direct in your follow-up in determining your status for the potential opportunity. The mistake most candidates make is that they leave the follow-up to the potential employer and never close the loop. In those cases, the initial meeting or interview was a waste of your time as you did not have a professional, persistent, and proactive follow-up plan.

NETIQUETTE

"Use social media for good and lift others up, not tear them down. Stay on the high road."

–Germany Kent

Who you are online is no different than who you are in person. Don't think for one second that one is more important than the other, but keep in mind that your online presence is becoming one of the most efficient ways to learn more about what you do and who you are in real life. Netiquette by definition is the correct or acceptable way of communicating on the internet. It is important to maintain a positive image online because your online presence can affect your personal and professional life. Here are some tips for maintaining a positive online image:

- Be respectful of others.
- Be mindful of what you post.
- Be aware of your audience.
- Be careful about what information you share.

- Be professional.
- Be yourself.

We have so much access to many different platforms to be ourselves, and it can become a slippery slope if not used in the proper manner. The increase in online usage will rise, and that being said, you must keep that in mind when you decide to navigate in your online communities. Psychologist and Professor at Royal Roads University, Elizabeth Hartney, captures it best by stating, "The golden rule of netiquette boils down to one basic guideline: Do not do or say online what you would not do or say offline." Here are some specific examples of how you can maintain a positive online image:

- Avoid posting offensive or discriminatory content.
- Be careful about what photos and videos you post.
- Think twice before commenting on someone else's post.
- Be aware of the privacy settings on your social media accounts.
- Only share information that you are comfortable sharing publicly.
- Be professional in your online communication, even if you are not at work.
- Be authentic and genuine in your online presence.

There are a few essential steps that can help you maintain a positive online image that will reflect well on you personally and professionally. If you want to go above and beyond, here are some additional things to keep in mind about netiquette:

- Once something is posted online, it is there forever. Be careful about what you say and do online, because it could come back to haunt you.

- Be aware of the power of social media. Social media can be a powerful tool for building relationships and sharing information, but it can also be used to spread hate and misinformation.
- Be mindful of your digital footprint. Everything you do online leaves a trace. Be careful about what you post, because it could be used against you in the future.

Being aware of netiquette can protect yourself and your reputation. To go even further, it can protect your brand and legacy. You would not want something you posted years ago to come back to haunt you, or your loved ones. No one is trying to dim your light or take away your right to the First Amendment, but words are powerful and can be used to help and harm you. Be smart, think, and type responsibly.

Hartney, E. (2023, June 28). *10 Basic Netiquette Rules*. Very Well Mind. https://www.verywellmind.com/ten-rules-of-netiquette-22285

LEVERAGE LINKEDIN

"LinkedIn is no longer an online resume.
It's your digital reputation."

–Jill Rowley

"LinkedIn, when used correctly, can become a catalyst for career change," wrote Kate Jones. That statement is as true now as it's ever been. For many years, LinkedIn served mostly as a platform for connecting with other professionals. Someone would invite you to connect and you would respond and typically, that was the end of the conversation. Many then turned LinkedIn into a game to see how many connections they could amass. Now, LinkedIn has become such a powerful online platform that even Gen Z, those born starting in 1997, are recognizing its value as much as Instagram and TikTok from a social perspective. There are approximately 500,000 recruiters on LinkedIn daily working to identify candidates to fill jobs. In a LinkedIn blog post from several years ago, titled, "Change Is In The Air: 7 LinkedIn Tips For Career Changers," Lindsay Pollack offered seven ways to leverage LinkedIn for those in a career transition:

#1: Become an expert on the career you want to pursue

#2: Optimize your LinkedIn profile for your new career

#3: Join LinkedIn groups related to your career

#4: Alert your network to your career change plans

#5: Talk to anyone who works or has worked in the field you want to join

#6: Sign up for LinkedIn job alerts

#7: Make real world changes

The bottom line, LinkedIn is one of your owned media channels. You are the researcher, writer, editor, and publisher. You have the ability to be read and heard by as many influencers as you choose. From mobilizing substantive connections to authoring and publishing thought leadership content, you must fully leverage LinkedIn. Jones concluded her post, writing, "Changing career direction can feel overwhelming, but it doesn't have to be. By taking the time to consider the relevant skills you've already honed, you will be able to smoothly pivot in a new direction. LinkedIn provides a ton of powerful tools to help you on your journey. With a well-targeted profile, you'll position yourself to make the change you desire."

Jones, K. (2017, October 12). *How To Use LinkedIn To Support A Career Change*. Career Enlightenment . https://careerenlightenment.com/use-linkedin-support-career-change

Lindsey Pollack. (2011, June 7). *Change Is In The Air: 7 LinkedIn Tips For Career Changers*. LinkedIn. https://blog.linkedin.com/2011/06/07/7-linkedin-tips-for-career-changers

CASH IN YOUR FAVOR BANK

*"We secure our friends not by accepting favors
but by doing them."*

–Thucydides

Throughout your lifetime, you have not maintained an Excel spreadsheet detailing all the good deeds you have done for others, but you have helped many in your professional and social network, and now is the time to cash in on that favor bank. While the idea of the "favor bank" became part of our lexicon after it was introduced by Tom Wolfe in 1987 in *The Bonfire of the Vanities*, it is more relevant to you now more than ever in the midst of a career transition. Don Spetner writes, "The idea is that one should make 'deposits' into the favor bank, because inevitably it will be necessary to one day make a 'withdrawal.' It's an efficient and time-worn system. It's also one of the most effective engines for advancing a career." Borrowing from Spetner, the favor bank is also one of the most effective engines for successfully completing your career transition. Now is the opportune time to take more than a moment to think of all the favors and acts of kindness you provided throughout your lifetime and your career to former colleagues, clients, classmates and vendors. Those individuals will be even more eager to support and assist you when you reach out to them to make a withdrawal. You can't take your favor bank with you when you leave this earth so start to spend some of that savings you accumulated because there is no better time than the present to cash in your favor bank.

Spetner, D. (2018, January 8). *The Favor Bank*. USC Annenberg School for Communication and Journalism. https://annenberg.usc.edu/research/center-public-relations/usc-annenberg-relevance-report/favor-bank

MOBILIZE THE MASSES

"The successful networkers I know, the ones receiving tons of referrals and feeling truly happy about themselves, continually put the other person's needs ahead of their own."

–Bob Burg

As previously highlighted in this book, it is critical to take time to brand yourself and get your resume and LinkedIn profile updated as well as identify your target companies. However, once these items are complete, it is essential that you leverage every channel that is available to you, mobilize your connections and network like you have never networked before. Here is a list of some resources you must leverage:

- Friends
- Family
- Former Co-workers
- Former Classmates
- Former Teammates

- Neighbors
- Industry & Professional Associations/Groups
- Executive Recruiters
- Alumni Associations
- Vendor Contacts
- Former Consultants you engaged and/or worked with
- Government resources – unemployment, retraining/ reskilling, etc.
- Fellow members of groups to which you belong
- Seek out and join and attend local job search and networking group meetings (check out meetup.com and other networking groups via sites like LandingExpert. com where a free comprehensive listing of networking groups can be found under Networking)
- Seek out and attend industry meetings, expo events and conferences

UNDERSTAND MENTOR VS. SPONSOR

"The delicate balance of mentoring someone is not creating them in your own image but giving them the opportunity to create themselves."

–Steven Spielberg

We learn the importance of a mentor and how effective they can be as you continue to grind it out in your career and personal endeavors, but a sponsor can be just as effective, if not more when it comes to career growth.

A mentor is someone who provides guidance and support to a less experienced person, typically in their career. Mentors typically have more experience and knowledge than their mentees, and they can offer advice, feedback, and encouragement. Mentors can also help mentees to develop their skills and knowledge, and to network with other people in their field.

A sponsor is someone who advocates for the advancement of another person's career. Sponsors typically have influence and power in their organization, and they can use their connections to help their protégés get promoted, get access to opportunities, and get their work noticed. Sponsors can also provide financial support to their protégés, such as paying for training or education.

Understand that there is no limit to the number of mentors and sponsors you can have but be strategic when recruiting them. These professionals will play an important role in most of your life decisions, inside and outside of the office. When explaining the difference, Maggie Wooll, thought partner and author wrote, "For one, mentors don't necessarily work in the same organization as you. But sponsors usually do." Being able to have reliable individuals to lean on inside and outside of your organization will allow you to constantly continue to grow, both personally and professionally, in very strategic ways.

Wooll, M. (2021, September 23). *Mento vs Sponsor: Why Having Both Is Key For Your Career*. Better Up. https://www.betterup.com/blog/mentor-vs-sponsor

RAPIDLY EXPAND YOUR NETWORK

*"Pulling a good network together takes effort,
sincerity and time."*

–Alan Collins

There are a number of ways you can rapidly expand your network. Identify a list of individuals to target to add as contacts to grow your network. On LinkedIn, there are individuals who have self-identified themselves as LinkedIn Open Networker (referred to as LION's or simply Open Networker) as they are open to connecting with you. As you are looking at companies you are targeting, see if anyone there is a LION or Open Networker. Connect with former coworkers and fellow college alums. You can find these individuals quicker by using the LinkedIn search feature with filters set properly to help identify these individuals. LinkedIn supplies a functionality where you can upload your contacts from an email program like Outlook or Google Mail and it will automatically find their matching LinkedIn profile and send an invitation to them to connect with you on LinkedIn. When you are networking, always seek to be introduced and connected by your point-of-contact with two more individuals who you can follow-up with – these can be two recruiters, two individuals at companies you are targeting, two members who are involved in networking groups you are looking to join or attend and on and one. The trick is to make the most of each interaction and constantly be multiplying by two or more and growing your network along the way as you have these interactions.

CONTENT IS KING: START BLOGGING, POSTING & PODCASTING

"Power doesn't come from content; power comes from the content that moves."

–Mark Schaefer

"Content is King" may date back to a 1996 essay Bill Gates wrote for the Microsoft web site, but it is even more applicable in 2024 and beyond especially for those who are in a career transition. There is no rule that states content can only be created and distributed by leading companies, brands and marketing agencies. Every single individual has the ability, skill and power to produce engaging and compelling thought leadership content that can not only be viewed, followed and shared, but also lead to that next career opportunity. Two of our favorite examples are Geno Schellenberger founder and host of the *Breaking & Entering* podcast who leveraged his podcast to launch his career in public relations and advertising, and Michael Rasile who launched the podcast, *For The Love of Sports*, which led to authoring his book, *Winning In Sports Business*, which resulted in securing jobs in his target industry, sports business. Once you identify the industry or category where you want to demonstrate and share thought leadership, there are two easy ways to get started. First, via LinkedIn, make a daily or weekly commitment to research and share content that is relevant to the industry and organizations you are prospecting. Each morning after you wake-up, conduct a simple Google search and share relevant industry news and provide commentary and analysis for select news. Also, on LinkedIn and other channels, follow as many individuals as possible who are influencers in the industry and organizations where you want to work. That same content you post on LinkedIn can then be amplified via your other owned media channels. Finally, go one step further in your content production and distribution efforts and use a platform like Wix, Squarespace, Hubspot, Go Daddy or any of the many do-it-yourself web sites or blog sites and create your own web site and blog that focuses exclusively on the industry and organizations where you want to take your talents. Once you have your sites up and running, share thought leadership content consistently. You should be writing thought-provoking, pithy posts that are highly sharable. All these actions take time, but ultimately, they will save you time making your job search more efficient. For a column for The Muse titled, "How My Personal Website Helped Me Land My Dream Job," Erin Greenawald wrote, "By getting yourself a URL and filling your site with keywords related to your field, you flip job searching on its head. No longer will you just be reaching out to recruiters—there's a better chance they'll find you through searches and reach out to you on their own." As Erin writes, by taking a content-centric approach, you just flipped your job search from reactive to proactive where potential employers will be reaching out to you.

Greenawald, E. (2021, March 5). *How My Personal Website Helped Me Land My Dream Job*. The Muse. https://www.themuse.com/advice/how-my-personal-website-helped-me-land-my-dream-job

SHAKE UP YOUR SOCIAL MEDIA

"Success on social media platforms, including LinkedIn, relies on your ability to make true connections."

–Kim Garst

No longer think of Facebook, Instagram and TikTok as purely just social media sites to share fun photos from your vacation or your date night with your significant other. Go beyond LinkedIn and use your social media channels to socialize your career transition. In an article for The Muse titled, "45 Things To Do On Social Media To Find Jobs," Erin Greenawald writes, "most people know how to use social media in their personal lives, but it actually has a lot of power to make (or break) your job search. Studies have shown that 92 percent of companies are using social media for hiring – and that three out of four hiring managers will check out a candidate's social profiles." Once word gets out that you are in between jobs, formally announce it on your social media channels. You never know who in your social media following may be the connector to your next opportunity. There are five times as many people on Facebook as there are on LinkedIn. Always keep your posts positive and even inspiring and motivating for your followers. As you participate in career networking group meetings or travel to new towns and locations for informal meetings and interviews, share your journey, quotes that may have inspired you and any learnings in a way that can positively impact your followers. Your social media channels are your owned media channels. You are the content creator, editor and publisher which means you have the power to socialize your career transition as you see fit... and believe us, the more engaging content you share, the more opportunities you will uncover.

Greenawald, E. (2020, June 18). *45 Things To Do On Social Media To Find Jobs*. The Muse. https://www.themuse.com/advice/45-things-to-do-on-social-media-to-find-jobs

CONNECT WITH A CAREER SUPPORT GROUP

"Opportunities don't happen, you create them."

–Chris Grosser

"To enhance their job search and make it more effective, many people are turning to the encouragement found in job clubs (or career support groups) for support, networking and sharing tips on job hunting, resume writing and interviewing. Many people find job clubs energizing and genuinely helpful in moving their job search forward." For example, if you reside in central New Jersey, specifically in Monmouth County, you live less than a one-hour drive from no less than five career support groups who meet weekly or monthly on different days. In other words, there are many career support networking groups nationwide who are eager to have you attend their meetings, share your story and learn from their guest speakers and career and job prospecting experts. You will even learn from former members who have successfully secured a job and return to the meetings to share the secrets to their success.

Even outside the in-person or Zoom meetings, the groups are sharing information and insights via their web site, Facebook platform and LinkedIn channel. The Breakfast Club NJ, which started with two people having breakfast more than 20 years ago to discuss job searches has blossomed to more than 6,000 members, shares no fewer than 25-35 job openings each week with its members via their direct email system. Most importantly, career support groups offer an army of like-minded individuals to help you on your journey which will feel lonely at times. These groups provide camaraderie, assistance, inspiration and motivation when you need it most. Simultaneously, your professional network will expand significantly, and you will learn and transform personally and professionally with each meeting you attend. No one gets a reward for securing their next job on their own. Instead, join one or more career support groups and expedite your journey to your next opportunity while making new friends in the process. Please go to http:// LandingExpert.com to see a lengthy list of job search and career networking groups.

Rasico, A. (2020, October 5). *Job Search Support Groups*. Circa. https://jobs. localjobnetwork.com/employment-resources/detail/job-search- support-groups/11392

SECURE SIDE GIGS

"You can't use up creativity. The more you use, the more you have."

–Maya Angelou

"Side gigs – no matter what form they take – are becoming a smart move both financially and career-wise." In today's society, side gigs are not a bad thing. They are actually becoming more popular with each passing year. We have heard of companies who encourage their employees to pursue side hustles. There are probably more people in your personal and professional network that drive for Uber or Lyft or deliver for DoorDash and Uber Eats as a side hustle than you even know. A side gig could be even more relevant to your career than driving for a ride sharing program. Just because you are looking for your next full-time opportunity doesn't mean you can't serve as a consultant in your industry or take on special projects at the exact same time. Consulting will keep your mind sharp and place you into an environment of collaboration with a larger team while adding more professional contacts that could be missing puzzle pieces to your search. There are many stories of individuals who were let go from their company and started consulting to pay the bills until they realized the consulting projects were paying the bills better than their full-time job while offering greater work-life balance. Other side gigs could include adjunct teaching at your local college or writing for an industry trade web site. Mark Beal, one of the authors of this book, has witnessed more of his recent college students who have graduated are immersed in two or three revenue generation occupations including one fulltime job as well as consulting and a side hustle. In other words, while your primary job is to secure your next job, don't do it in a vacuum with your blinders on. Instead, multi-task and secure side gigs to not only pay some bills, but to create more connections towards that next opportunity. If you do engage in a side gig while you are employed, ensure that it doesn't present a conflict of intertest to your primary employment.

Bitte, R. (2020, June 19). *4 Questions Smart People Ask About Side Gigs (So They Don't Lose Their Jobs)*. The Muse. https://www.themuse.com/advice/4-questions-smart-people-ask-about-side-gigs-so-they-dont-lose-their-jobs

BUILD A BRIDGE WITH A BRIDGE JOB

"If you are not willing to risk the unusual, you will have to settle for the ordinary."

–Jim Rohn

A s you advance in your career, not every job needs to serve the same purpose as the previous job. Based on your life stage, age, retirement savings and a number of other factors, bridge jobs could serve as a solution, or they could bridge to entirely new opportunities. In a March 1, 2023 article authored by Andrew Seaman for *Get Hired by LinkedIn News*, he writes, "Bridges get people over gaps. Similarly, bridge jobs help people overcome a gap in their careers. Maybe they were recently laid off or quit. Maybe they need money. Maybe they just want to be around new people. Whatever the reason, bridge jobs are incredible tools that often go underutilized." *U.S. News & World Report* writes, "people may be interested in looking for 'bridge jobs,' work opportunities that keep them busy (and making money) while allowing them to ease slowly into retirement." The article continues, "Bridge jobs are obviously helpful to older individuals who want to keep working. But they're also beneficial to employers, more of whom recognize the value of hiring and retaining experienced employees..." Use a transition in your career, whether planned or unplanned, to explore all opportunities – freelance (Upwork, Fiverr, etc.), consulting, starting your own business and even bridge jobs. It is opportunities like bridge jobs that keep you highly productive and highly collaborative while introducing you to more individuals who become part of your network and could serve as connectors to future opportunities.

Seaman, A. (2023, March 1). *How To Find A Bridge Job*. LinkedIn. https://www.linkedin.com/pulse/how-find-bridge-job-get-hired-by-linkedin-news/

Brooks, R. (2020, May 22). *How To Find A Bridge Job Second Career*. U.S. News & World Report. https://money.usnews.com/money/retirement/second-careers/articles/how-to-find-a-bridge-job-second-career

FREELANCING CAN BECOME FULL-TIME

"A goal is not always meant to be reached;
it often is simply as something to aim at."

–Bruce Lee

"Whether you're doing minimal, part-time freelance projects for this client, or you're working close to a full-time schedule as their freelancer, there are several concrete steps you can take to turn a freelance client into a full-time employer," writes Brie Weiler Reynolds for a column titled, "How To Transition From Freelance Work To A Full-Time Position." Ultimately, you have your sights set on a full-time job with full-time pay and full-time benefits, but while you are searching for that opportunity, don't reject invitations to be a freelancer. "If there is one thing I would have done differently during my transition, I would have put myself 'out there' for freelance work. Once I made that approach an important part of my weekly career transition routine, it started to pay dividends. I formed my own LLC as a result and it potentially could lead to consulting being a full-time endeavor," said Keith Green, a marketing/public relations executive and university professor. Freelancing can put you right in the middle of an organization where you have the opportunity to immerse yourself in the business of a company while demonstrating that you can deliver value that drives business impact. Additionally, freelancing, like a bridge job, will introduce you to a significant number of new professional contacts who could serve as a connection point to your next full-time opportunity. Earlier in this book, we invited readers to change the rules in 2024 and beyond and it relates to jobs and careers. In a May 21, 2023 article for *CNBC*, Gili Malinsky reports that, "Generation Z is making its way into the workplace, and many members are rethinking the traditional nine-to-five." Malinsky cites a 2023 Fiverr survey in which 70 percent of Gen Zers consider freelancing an alternative to a traditional fulltime office job.

Reynolds, B. W. (2015, April 29). *How to Transition from Freelance Work to a Full Time Position*. Lifehacker. https://lifehacker.com/how-to-transition-from-freelance-work-to-a-full-time-po-1700762612

Malinsky, G. (2023, May 21). *3 Gen Zers on deciding to become full-time freelancers: 'I wouldn't go back' to a corporate job*. CNBC. https://www.cnbc.com/2023/05/21/majority-of-gen-z-considers-freelancing-to-be-a-viable-career-option.html

GET CERTIFIED

"The beautiful thing about learning is that nobody can take it away from you."

–B.B. King

In a March 4, 2023 article in *The Economic Times* titled "The growing importance of 'skills-first' credentials in career progression," Debleena Majumdar writes, "In today's world, education is no longer a linear process. Which meant X years of school followed by Y years of college and Z years of work. The need to keep our skills updated is an ongoing need today and hence educational degrees and certificates play a role at various points in our life." Certifications can help your candidacy. They demonstrate an assessment of one's level of competency in a given area or discipline by an independent authority. Just carefully look at the many certifications out there and limit your pursuit of certifications to those that would be most relevant to the job you are seeking. Perhaps go to a site like Indeed.com and pull some job requisitions that are consistent with the opportunity that you are seeking. Look across these job requisitions and see if any of them list certifications as required or suggested for the candidates that they are seeking. Now, it is getting easier to obtain certifications as many original equipment manufacturers (OEMs) that offer certifications in their products, services, and/or methodologies are now offering certification materials and tests for free via online training sites like Alison.com and among Massive Open Online Courses "MOOC." Several universities even offer the content from their courses for free to the public. Check with those who are established in your profession, your alumni office, former managers you reported to and solicit their thoughts if they feel certifications would be beneficial and if so, which ones in particular would be of help to you and your specific career goals.

Majumdar, D. (2023, March 4). *The Growing Importance Of "Skills-First" Credentials In Career Progression.* Economic Times. https://economictimes.indiatimes.com/jobs/fresher/the-role-of-industry-micro-credentials-in-higher-education/articleshow/98406405.cms?from=mdr

RECRUIT RECRUITERS

*"Be curious. Use data. Leverage imagination.
Be an expert. Be an enthusiast. Be authentic.
Know your competition."*

–Jim Stroud

If only we had a penny from every job seeker who we encountered who was frustrated with a recruiter, or that they didn't call them back, or give them the time they felt they deserved, we would be enjoying retirement on a beach somewhere. The truth is that time is money to recruiters, and they must use it wisely in order to hit metrics that measure their performance and drive the recruiter's compensation. Stephanie Sparks captures the recruiter-candidate relationship well in a June 22, 2023 article for *Jobvite*. "As the labor market and record-low unemployment rates keep recruiters on their toes, the focus on the candidate experience continues. The candidate experience includes all the feelings, impressions, interactions, and activities a job seeker encounters along their candidate journey. It's how a candidate feels they've been treated throughout the recruitment process and how that treatment makes them feel about the organization." There are several techniques that you, the candidate, can use that will help build your emotional bank accounts with those you are networking with while at the same time helping you establish a strong relationship with recruiters. Previously in this book, you were advised to join professional job search and networking groups. These groups can help you with recruiters in a number of ways. First, ask those that you meet in the networking groups to suggest to you who they feel are the top recruiters and even ask if they would be willing to make an introduction to the recruiter on your behalf. Also, once you are speaking with the recruiter here is a technique that is a win/win for you, the recruiter, and those in your network. When speaking with the recruiter, ask them if they have a hard-to-fill position. Tell the recruiter you are a member of several networking groups and would be willing to distribute this hard-to-fill opportunity to your groups to help out the recruiter. The recruiter gets additional resource(s) to fill a tough-to-fill job opportunity and those you are networking with now have additional opportunities. Next time you call that recruiter to check on your candidacy they will be more willing to take your call and push for you as a candidate as you've gone above and beyond and helped them.

Sparks, S. (2023, September 18). *Candidate Expectations You Need to Know in 2024*. Jobvite. https://www.jobvite.com/blog/candidate-expectations/

ENLIST THE SUPPORT OF A CAREER COACH

"A good coach can change a game. A great coach can change a life."

–John Wooden

As you are managing your opportunities, you need to do some analysis to determine what your strengths and weaknesses are so you can determine where you need to improve and if you may need some help doing so.

- Are you not getting interviews? You may benefit from engaging a career coach that specializes in improving your resume and/or branding. Also, you may want to attend networking group sessions specific to this aspect of job search.

- Are you not getting offers following interviews? You may benefit from engaging a career coach that specializes in improving your interviewing competency.

- Are recruiters not calling you back? You need to rethink how you are leveraging and interfacing with recruiters in your job search.
- Are you effectively using references? You need to work well with your references:
  - o Gain their agreement to serve as a reference on your behalf
  - o Review any opportunity that you will provide them as a reference in advance recapping the opportunity, who it is with, and why you would make a great candidate
  - o Keep them informed through each stage of the process so they understand and can be prepared and anticipating the contact reaching out
  - o Remember to thank them for their support regardless of the outcome and offer to reciprocate on their behalf if ever needed

If you consider engaging a career coach:

- Be clear on fees and what the service will consist of in tangible terms
- Request some references and/or ask for coach recommendations from your network
- Ask the coach what they specialize in and why you should select and collaborate with them

PART IV

Think & Act Strategically
To Achieve Job Search Success

BE A SEVEN PERCENTER

"Network continually – 85 percent of all jobs are filled through contacts and personal references."

–Brian Tracy

"According to the University of Michigan University Career Center, referrals account for just 7% of all job applicants but 40% of all hires." Take a few moments to comprehend that powerful statistic. The majority of your competition who are applying for the same job that you are targeting are simply submitting their resumes online and hoping that someone calls them for an interview. But always remember, "Hope is not a strategy." Instead, be a seven percenter. In other words, take all the lessons in this book in an effort to be referred and recommended for an opportunity you are strategically targeting. Simple math will tell you that you do not want to be a 93 percenter. Andrew Seaman reinforces this in his post for LinkedIn Get Hired when he writes, "Employee referrals are often thought to be the proverbial golden tickets of job seeking. While they don't guarantee a job, they can increase the odds that your application will be seen by a recruiter or hiring manager and ultimately give you a boost in the hiring process. An employee referral is essentially an endorsement within a potential employer of you and your talents for a specific position." Referrals not only provide you a much better statistical chance of securing the job, but it also helps you bypass the dreaded ATS robots and advances you directly to the phase of the candidate screenings and interviews where you can demonstrate your case for the job via old school human interaction (H.I.). As we have highlighted in this book, no matter how technologically advanced the employee recruiting process has become, companies, big and small, still rely on human interaction to vet and select the winning candidate which is one reason why referrals often help secure the position in the end.

Klazema, M. (2016a, October 18). *8 Ways You Can Increase Your Chances Of Getting Hired*. PNP Staffing Group. https://pnpstaffinggroup.com/8-ways-can-increase-chances-getting-hired/

Seaman, A. (2020, October 5). *Why Referrals Are Powerful Job Search Tools*. LinkedIn. https://www.linkedin.com/pulse/why-referrals-powerful-job-search-tools-andrew-seaman/

IT'S NOT WHO YOU KNOW, IT'S WHO THEY KNOW

"It's not who you know. It's who they know."

–Stan Phelps

I am sure we are all familiar with the expression, "It's not what you know, but who you know." Martin Howard reinforces this notion when he writes, "Over the past number of years, I've learned to embrace that landing a job has very little to do with what I know. It doesn't matter that I have an MBA, that I'm a certified Project Management Professional (PMP), a certified Lean Six Sigma Black Belt (LSSBB), or a Certified Scrum Master (CSM). For me, none of that has helped to land a single job. Instead, every position I *have* landed was because I knew someone on that team. I realize that it truly is about who you know and who knows you." This is very true, especially when you find yourself searching and prospecting for your next job. However, IBM Futurist, TEDx speaker and best-selling author of the "goldfish" series of books regarding delivering optimal service to customers and employees, Stan

Phelps, takes it one step further. Stan likes to say to those seeking their career opportunity, "It's not who you know. It's who they know." Stan's insightful expression captures the essence of LinkedIn. To truly leverage the power of LinkedIn is not simply to connect with your connections, but it's to have your connections ultimately connect you to their connections who are already working at companies that you are targeting and prospecting or at least external vendors and agencies who conduct business with those organizations. Like any winning chess player, strategically think several moves ahead with the goal of checkmating your opponent. In your case, checkmating means utilizing your pieces, your immediate personal and professional contacts, to logically connect you to as many as five or six other connections that will lead you to a hiring manager or the recruiter in the human resources department of the employer you are looking to be employed by. Ultimately, you want these new connections to think of you when a new opportunity arises. Set your vision well beyond your immediate contacts and you will set yourself up for success.

Howard, M. (2021, December 6). *It's Who You Know, Not What You Know.* Medium. https://medium.com/@martinghoward/its-who-you-know-not-what-you-know-2859fb546805

CREATE YOUR OWN WORD CLOUD

*"All successful men and women are big dreamers.
They imagine what their future could be, ideal in every
respect, and then they work every day toward their
distant vision, that goal or purpose."*

–Brian Tracy

As businesses and organizations do each and every day to visualize customer sentiment or the attitudes of their employees, design your own career transition word cloud, sometimes called a text cloud or tag cloud, to help you visualize any number of topics relevant to your job search. One of your word clouds could be a visual representation of your strengths and areas for improvement. Another word cloud could be a mapping of your top-20 target companies and organizations with the largest fonts representing your top-five or 10 prospects where you have the greatest number of connections. A third word cloud could consist of a side-by-side comparison of the skills and experiences that you highlight in your resume and LinkedIn profile compared to the requisites that are featured in the job opening description. Lisa

Lepki writes, "Word clouds are fun to use as a visual aid... to underscore the keywords on which you're focusing." Consider a word cloud another tool in your arsenal to leverage that can help you visualize the communication and messaging that you are using in writing and verbally to successfully secure the next opportunity in your career.

Lepki, L. (2020, December 20). *How Do You Create A Word Cloud?*. Pro Writing Aid. https://prowritingaid.com/art/425/What-the-Heck-is-a-Word-Cloud-and-Why-Would-I-Use-One.aspx

UNDERSTAND WHAT YOU'VE DONE, NOT WHERE YOU DID IT

"Take time to gather up the past so that you will be able to draw from your experience and invest them in the future."

–Jim Rohn

Too often, too many job seeking candidates prioritize the industry or category they worked in, and not the actual work they did, the successes they achieved, the business-building solutions they implemented and the skills they applied. Most, if not all of those experiences are highly transferable to other industries. In fact, many companies today recognize the value in hiring individuals who can bring a fresh perspective from their past experience in a different industry. Place less of a focus on where you did your work and more of a focus on the work itself, your case studies, the measurable impact you and your team had on the business. While it may be obvious that an accountant in one industry can transfer those skills and be an accountant in another industry, other occupations may not appear so obvious. There was an individual who worked for a nationally recognized transportation and travel company where he arranged special charters, trips and other unique travel for major corporations and professional sports teams. As he journeyed through his transition, he was focused exclusively on working for a travel company. He limited potential opportunities by limiting his perspective on his experience and skills. Once the light bulb went off and he realized what he really did was logistics and coordination for large numbers of people, he came to the realization that he could apply that to a wide number of industries and organizations - conference and convention centers, stadiums and arenas, professional sports teams and major corporations. As you explore beyond the obvious on your journey, don't just look at where you worked, but delve deeper into what you actually did.

H.I. BEATS OUT A.I.

"Social media is an amazing tool, but it's really the face-to-face interaction that makes a long-term impact."

–Felicia Day

In a June 16, 2023 article for *CBS News*, Megan Cerullo writes, "Looking for a job? You may find yourself "face to face" with an artificial intelligence bot, rather than a person. Corporate recruiters have long used AI to quickly scan job applications and whittle down the number of applicants. Now, companies are increasingly using the technology to conduct the job interview itself. This presents job candidates with a range of new challenges in what can often be a stressful situation, not the least of which is this emerging consideration: How exactly do you impress a bot?" While each day, there are more articles and talk about Artificial Intelligence (A.I.) and ChatGPT, it is Human Interaction (H.I.) which will ultimately lead you to success in your career transition journey. One of the authors of this book, Mark Beal, expands upon that concept in a guest column he wrote for Dice.com. "No matter how innovative the hiring process has become with the infusion of Artificial Intelligence and Applicant Tracking Systems (ATS), Human Interaction (H.I.) will ultimately determine the candidates that get hired. Prior to the pandemic, the candidate screening process consisted of a series of in-person face-to-face interviews before the winning applicant was hired. Now, thanks to advancements in technology, most employers are using ATS robots to rank applicants based on specific terms they use in their resume or are employing interactive platforms such as LaunchPad (which combines video interviewing, mobile technology and intelligent automation). If a job candidate successfully passes that tech-vetting gauntlet, they may have earned the chance to be interviewed by a computer or a chatbot before they ever have any actual human contact. However, we believe going 'old school' and prioritizing human interaction in the job prospecting process will lead to greater success for job applicants. The odds of an individual getting a job via an online job site application which typically utilizes ATS is just 1 out of 250, according to a University of Michigan study. However, an individual can take more of a human interaction approach to job-seeking: employee referrals only make up seven percent of applications, but 40 percent of hires. In other words, if an applicant leverages their network, they will drastically improve their chances of securing a job than if they solely rely on today's tech innovations which are screening candidates and oftentimes eliminating the best person for the job."

Cerullo, M. (2023, June 16). *Your Next Job Interview Might Be With AI. Here's How To Ace It.* CBS News. https://www.cbsnews.com/news/ai-job-interview-tips-to-prepare-artificial-intelligence/

Beal, M. (2019b, April 26). *Human Interaction Beats A.I. In Getting Your First Job.* Dice. https://www.dice.com/career-advice/human-interaction-beats-ai-first-job

BYPASS THE ROBOTS

*"Know where you want to go and make sure
the right people know about it."*

–Meredith Mahoney

As highlighted in the previous lesson, the job application process has gone hi-tech with the proliferation of Applicant Tracking Systems (ATS). While you will formally need to apply to just about every job by submitting your resume via an online application portal that uses ATS robots, you need to counter that by making a human connection with someone at the company. "Often you may not know someone within a target organization to whom you can send your resume, but more times than not you can find a second connection there as long as you're willing to invest the time to look. A friend of a friend, a former colleague's client, a cousin's cousin... there's almost always a way to get your resume into someone's hands, outside of the online submission, and you'll increase your chances of getting an interview substantially if you're willing to look," commented Jim Sias, a leading marketing executive. Applying to jobs today requires a one-two punch combination, but most applicants only rely on the initial jab by submitting their resume online, and never follow-up with the counterpunch. It is the counterpunch of following-up your formal submission by reaching out to your network to learn who can make a call on your behalf to a decision maker on the inside that will enable you to bypass the robots. Time after time, the majority of individuals who get invited to be interviewed and ultimately win the job, know how to throw a powerful counter punch. Longtime human resources executive Liz Ryan provided a great glimpse behind the ATS curtain in a column she penned for Forbes titled, "How To Sneak Past The Online Application And Get The Job." Consider what she wrote as you submit your next application. "The people who staff the broken recruiting system, naturally, can't tell you 'Just go around the back way and forget the online application.' They're not allowed to say that. They have to say 'No, you must follow the rules,' but they know it's not true. Hiring managers have problems. They are desperate for talent. They don't want to receive a stack of resumes to review six to eight weeks after they run a job ad. They want to hire someone now! Why shouldn't they hire you?" As you get frustrated with ATS technology, remind yourself of the approach Liz Ryan recommends.

Ryan, L. (2016, August 3). *How To Sneak Past The Online Application And Get The Job*. Forbes. https://www.forbes.com/sites/lizryan/2015/08/03/how-to-sneak-past-the-online-application-and-get-the-job/?sh=1ee2c2e12299

ACHIEVE ATS SUCCESS

"Your resume is very likely to face off with an applicant tracking system before it reaches the desk of any human recruiter."

–Sarah K. White/Terena Bell

Applicant Tracking Systems (ATS) have numerous nuances that one must be aware of prior to submitting applications for jobs as there are many rules that if you are not aware, can keep your submittal from ever being seen by the potential employer so you will never even be considered. Large employers are more apt to use an ATS as it automates their ability to publicize their open positions and is an easy way to obtain a lot of candidates and they won't have to compensate a recruiter or other third party while also helping the employer be EEOC compliant.

The following is a list of a few of the top ATS solutions:

Taleo	Workday
Brassring	iCIMS
SmartRecruiters	JazzHR

If you're applying to a large firm, the probability is that you are doing so through an ATS. Also, if you are applying through an online form, you're more than likely doing so through an ATS. Even LinkedIn and Indeed use an ATS. Recruiters use ATS to filter resumes by searching for key skills and titles. The recruiters will craft a search so it can contain multiple terms. For example, they might perform a complex search that contains a combination of titles and skills to identify candidates for the job. You can reverse engineer keywords for your resume by doing a marketing analysis of identifying a dozen job requirements consistent with the opportunity you are seeking and identifying and reusing the words that the recruiters use in their job requirements. Resume formatting is critical to your success with an ATS. Keep section headings simple, use consistent formatting for your work history and dates, avoid tables, and use a .docx or .pdf file format. Understanding the requirements of an ATS and adhering to them when creating your "qualified submissions" is a great way to improve the success of your job search efforts.

MAKE QUALIFIED SUBMISSIONS

"Find out what you like doing best and get someone to pay you for doing it."

–Katharine Whitehorn

What is a qualified submission? A qualified submission includes the following steps:

Step 1 – Research and target a company.

Step 2 - Once a position is found that you are a strong candidate for and have strong interest in, you need to work your network aggressively to find someone at the target company to provide insight on the firm so you understand the culture, how levels work, related pay by level, and quite possibly get you an introduction directly into the hiring manager.

Step 3 – Make your case for your candidacy for the opportunity with your resume by factually reordering bullets, expanding or collapsing points as to their applicability to requirements of position so that clearly your experience, education and skills highlight that you meet the requirements as applicable

Step 4 – Create a T Letter (see the T Letter lesson) as part of your cover letter.

Completing these four steps so that you have a "qualified submission" takes time and it is hard work, but the job search is about quality, not quantity. If you take the time to perform the steps required of a qualified submission and strive to make at least one qualified submission a day you will be happy to see the positive results that you will have in the form of a number of interviews by following the formula and creating "qualified submissions." This will increase your probability of landing as quickly as you can and keeping you focused on those positions that you are qualified for at companies you are targeting because you are a cultural match.

MANAGE YOUR OPPORTUNITIES EFFECTIVELY

"In the middle of difficulty lies opportunity."

–Albert Einstein

If you approach your job search correctly, you should be juggling many opportunities at one time. The challenge is to transform from simply juggling to effectively managing those opportunities. You can use a shareware product or something as simple as Microsoft Excel that many of us already use for other projects. The approach for effectively managing your opportunities is simple:

Create a spreadsheet or database and make each column or field applicable to common information you need to manage each opportunity. Here are some suggestions for columns/ fields to get you going:

Name of Employer

Title of Position

Compensation Range

Date you found the job posted

Contact at Firm

Contact at Firm's Information (email, phone, etc.)

Version of Resume and Cover letter submitted

Networking contact for this Target Firm

Networking Contact's Information

Date for follow-up communication

Date you initiated your candidacy

Status: In progress, interview, interview completed, informed no longer being considered

Notes: Free form field of documenting each interaction with the employer, recruiter and other gatekeepers

MASTER TARGETING TECHNIQUES

"There is only one winning strategy. It is to carefully define the target market and direct a superior offering to that target market."

–Philip Kotler

So, you are about to embark on your job search journey. What's the first thing we do when we want to go on a trip? When we get into the car, the first thing we do is enter the coordinates for our destination in the GPS or an app such as Waze. In your job search, the coordinates for your destination are the companies that you are targeting. These are companies that you have spent quality time analyzing to determine that you have an interest in pursuing them as an employer. We refer earlier in this book to these companies as your top-20 targets. During a job search, the companies you target may change as you will become apprised of new employers that you may decide to add to your list of targeted companies and some firms may have to be removed from additional information learned (perhaps a recent bad earnings report and/or poor financial outlook for the firm, announcement of workforce reduction at the firm, etc.). Having a list of target companies will focus your job search efforts to those firms you are targeting so that your daily efforts are guided. It is also essential when networking as this will help members of your network assist you more effectively.

GO WHERE IT'S WARM

*"No cold calling. Ever. You should attempt
to sell only to warm leads."*

–Perry Marshall

Valerie Schlitt writes, "Warm leads have, at the very least, raised their hand and expressed interest in your offering. While warm leads vary in degrees of temperature, from lukewarm to borderline hot, they all have two things in common. One, they hold great potential for future sales. Two, they require nurturing and cultivation to keep them from turning cold again. Ideally, those warm leads will one day turn hot." If you have ever held a job in sales or had to lead the new business for your agency or organization, you always start with your warmest leads and prospects. In other words, as you identify and rank the companies that you want to prospect and target, prioritize those where you have the most connections inside the organization and outside in the form of external vendors and agencies. Consider other factors as well including your experience and skills versus the business model of the organization. For example, if you have had a career in consumer marketing and there is a company that is looking for a marketing veteran with a focus on business-to-business, that may not be the warmest lead even though it is a marketing role. Once you have identified your top-20 or 25 target companies to prospect, rank the companies based on a warm-to-cold spectrum. Review each company and consider a number of factors like those we mention in this lesson and rank the warmest prospects in your top-five. Those top-five prospects should be the ones that you invest the majority of your time and resources as these are your warmest leads.

Martins, A. (2023, July 28). *9 Lead Conversion Tips For Enhanced Success*. Business. https://www.business.com/articles/9-steps-to-lead-conversion-success/

TRANSFORM YOUR RESUME

"No one creates a perfect resume on their first try. Writing a perfect resume is a messy process, but the easiest way to start is by simply getting in the right mindset and putting pen to paper."

–Matthew T. Cross

If you are like the majority of people, you have not even looked at your resume since the last time you secured your last job. So, don't simply just blow the dust off it and add three new sub bullets for your latest experience. Instead, conduct some more research regarding resumes that are compelling and ultimately make the final cut. Most importantly, reach into your network and identify one or more contacts in human resources and recruiting. Individuals in these roles review hundreds of resumes weekly. We always like to say that when you ask 10 people for resume advice, you will receive 20 conflicting responses and conflicting directions Everyone has a take on the do's and don'ts of resume writing, but what should be included and the level of detail should be consistent with what is needed to successfully convey that you are a great candidate for the position being recruited for. They can quickly and effectively tell you how to transform your resume from a style and content perspective. Once you have applied their resume recommendations, email your resume to several decision makers in your network across a variety of industries. Since they may work in categories outside your expertise, you are looking for a gut reaction rather than the technical commentary you will receive from a recruiter. Always remember that your resume is a living and breathing document. It is never completed. For every job you apply to, you may tweak your resume to reflect and highlight relevant experience that is applicable to that specific job opening. In an article titled, "56 Resume Tips To Transform Your Job Search," Jon Shields emphasizes the importance of developing and maintaining a central resume that houses all your critical experience and information. "Consider maintaining a master resume or career management document. Think of this as a giant, overstuffed curriculum vitae (CV). It should contain all your job duties, all your accomplishments, all the tools that you used– everything you can think of for every job you've ever had. Maintaining a document like this can provide a great starting point for new resumes, ensuring that you don't forget anything important while allowing you to simply delete content rather than rewriting." A very important factor to your success is that the better your network, the lower the importance of your resume in the job search process. The reason for this, if you can arrange a recommendation from a resource that the hiring manager trusts directly, this is a critical factor towards increasing your probability of success in landing that opportunity. The reason this is critical is that as per Steven Covey, you are operating at the "Speed of Trust." Basically, you are tapping into the strength of the relationship that the individual who provided the recommendation has with the hiring manager. We have all heard that a recruiter or hiring manager literally spends seconds looking at resumes and determining who to submit as potential candidates. This also changes when a personal recommendation is involved. When revising your resume look to the future, not to the past, unless it is relevant to the opportunity you are seeking. While looking to the future some may include using ChatGPT to write their resume. We prefer the approach offered by Entrepreneur in a July 19, 2023 article titled. "Exploring the 6 Different Types of Resumes." The article states, "The right resume format doesn't just present your qualifications but does so in a manner that aligns with your career goals and the specific job you're targeting."

Nunez, J. (2023, June 21). *60 Resume Tips To Help You Land Interviews.* Jobscan. https://www.jobscan.co/resume-tips

Staff, E. (2023, July 19). *Exploring the 6 Different Types of Resumes.* https://www.entrepreneur.com/living/exploring-the-6-different-types-of-resumes/455545

HAVE MULTIPLE RESUMES

"The shorter and plainer the better."

–Beatrix Potter

While having a comprehensive resume that chronicles your entire work history is valuable, crafting multiple tailored resumes for specific job applications can be a game-changer. When recruiters sift through a multitude of resumes, they seek commonalities and transferable skills relevant to the target position. Suppose you're transitioning from a sales role to a marketing position. In that case, it's pivotal to meticulously review the job description and customize your qualifications to align with the hiring team's expectations. This approach greatly enhances your chances of standing out and securing your desired role in a competitive job market. The practice of tailoring your resume for specific job applications is a strategic move that can significantly enhance your prospects in the competitive job market. Just as a craftsman selects the right tools for each project, customizing your resume demonstrates your readiness to meet the unique demands of each role. By aligning your qualifications and experiences with the job requirements, you not only stand out in the eyes of recruiters but also showcase your adaptability and commitment to securing the position. It's a powerful tool that can help you craft a compelling narrative of your suitability for the role, ultimately increasing your chances of success in your job search.

UNDERSTAND DATA & DETAIL
FOR LINKEDIN & RESUME

"We are surrounded by data, but starved for insights."

–Jay Baer

Your LinkedIn profile and your resume are two very separate artifacts critical to your job search and should be complementary but not contain information at the same level of detail. Please take notice that most employers will now conduct a digital search of your information and if the digital data contradicts what is on your resume it could result in the employer eliminating you from consideration for the position. Also, LinkedIn has more than 500,000 recruiters who are searching for candidates for jobs that they are seeking to fill so it is critical you understand how they use the product and present your information in such a way so you are easily found by the recruiters and seen as a match for the positions that they are recruiting for.

How should your LinkedIn profile and resume be similar?

Your LinkedIn profile should be complementary to your resume in that it should reconcile to your resume at a higher level of detail. You should have the same jobs, job titles, in the same timeframe between the two artifacts, however, the level of detail supporting your explanation of the responsibilities at the position should be high level on LinkedIn but more detailed and in the PARs format (Lesson 93) on your resume.

How should your LinkedIn profile and resume be dissimilar?

On LinkedIn, there is a prescribed format for the profile and there are additional attributes to your profile (skills, endorsements, recommendations, awards) that exist that aren't present on your resume that you want to exploit to your advantage in your LinkedIn profile. Carefully choose those data items that will help recruiters identify you as a potential match for the position they are seeking to fill.

GO BACK TO SCHOOL

"The most successful people in life are the ones who ask questions. They're always learning. They're always growing. They're always pushing."

–Robert Kiyosaki

All of a sudden if you are in between jobs, you have some time on your hands. Don't waste it. Instead, go ahead and do some of those things you pushed off, but never had the time. In today's online world of education, going back to school can take on many forms. It can be as simple as logging on to a one-time only webinar taught by an author, actor or athlete. It could mean getting that certificate in search engine optimization (SEO) or some other subject matter that will bolster your resume and improve your chances of securing your next opportunity. It could mean attending a guest lecture being given by a power player in your industry and meeting that individual may bridge the gap to a company you are targeting. Or, it could mean earning a mini MBA or a master's degree while you simultaneously seek your next opportunity. It could even mean going back to school to serve as an adjunct professor at a local community college or university where you can leverage your career experiences while potentially launching a new career in education which many people have accomplished as part of their own career transition. Nicole Fallon writes, "It's never too late to change career paths. If you're not happy, you deserve the chance to take a different road – no matter what that entails. For some career changers, this means returning to school." Whatever the reason, be a student for life and let new learnings and lessons take you places you never imagined. Continuous learning has never been as important as it is now given the unprecedented pace of change and volume of change that we are experiencing.

Bushnell, M. (2023, February 21). *What You Need to Know About Going Back to School for a Career Change*. Business News Daily. https://www.businessnewsdaily.com/7064-back-to-school-career-change.html

THINK BIG &
START A SMALL BUSINESS

"A big business starts small."

–Sir Richard Branson

"People are not born entrepreneurs. They normally become one after a problem is presented to them. Some are trying to solve a common issue we face, while some are trying to change the world. Throughout my entrepreneurial journey, one of the most common catalysts I have found for entrepreneurship has been associated with job loss." Mike Wood wrote this for *Entrepreneur* after losing his job and starting his own marketing agency. Depending on a number of critical factors include your life stage, the amount of money you have invested, your age in relation to the number of years you want to work, your passions outside your day job and many others, you don't necessarily have to transition from one job to another job. You can transition from a job to your own business. One example is a longtime public relations veteran in the real estate industry who was impacted by a corporate downsizing and consolidation. While his first reaction was to find his next job, as he immersed himself in his transition, he realized that he could leverage his many years as a public relations and communication specialist in real estate and launch his own public relations agency. Several years later, his agency is thriving, and he is enjoying greater work-life balance than he did when he worked full-time for a large corporation. If you are in a position to do so, seriously consider leveraging your past experiences as well as your passions and hobbies and start your own small business or consultancy. Use this opportunity to set your own rules and write your own business plan and determine your company's own visions and mission.

Wood, M. (2016, August 26). *Lost Your Job? Consider it a Wake-Up Call to Become an Entrepreneur.* Entrepreneur. https://www.entrepreneur.com/leadership/lost-your-job-consider-it-a-wake-up-call-to-become-an/280636

EXERCISE YOUR ENTREPRENEURIAL SPIRIT

"Don't limit yourself. Many people limit themselves to what they think they can do. You can go as far as your mind lets you. What you believe, remember, you can achieve."

–Mary Kay Ash

For many years, you have relied on a larger power to pay your salary and benefits. You have leaned on big business or perhaps a small business to survive. Can you imagine a world where you generate your own revenue and you don't rely on an employer to help you pay your bills? You and you alone can control your own destiny by exercising your entrepreneurial spirit. There are millions of individuals who have left Corporate America and who have started their own business and ignored the doubters who told them it would be impossible. A business does not have to be a traditional brick and mortar store. In today's digital world, a business can be launched and sustained in the smallest room in your house using a mobile phone, personal computer and your entrepreneurial mindset. Before you race to your next job, evaluate all your options and seriously consider mobilizing all the experience, expertise and intellectual capital you have accumulated to support your own company or consultancy. David Siroty, a senior public relations and marketing executive shared his inspirational story. "When I was downsized from my job – something that Corporate America seems to love doing to all of us – a friend who owned his own business doubted my ability to start my own consultancy. He didn't think I had the entrepreneurial spirit or the guts to do it. I did it. I am now in my third year of leading my own company. No one is secure anymore, but now I control my own destiny and I realize that there is plenty of fun and interesting work out there for me to handle and make a nice income in the process."

CONTINUE TO SERVE OTHERS

"Your purpose in life is to use your gifts and talents to help other people. Your journey in life teaches you how to do that."

–Tom Krause

"I heard a famous music industry executive say in an interview that if you are in the service business, you always need to be of service," remarked PJ Brovak, a marketing communications veteran. "That rang true to me not only in my profession, but during my search. You would be amazed how the people responded to my willingness to put them first." While your journey to your next job opportunity should be your primary focus throughout your transition, part of that focus can include assisting others in your professional and personal network who will call on you because of your skills, experiences and relationships. It may seem odd that they are asking for your service knowing you are out-of-work and seeking your next job, but serving them is all part of a proactive mindset and approach as you never know what your service may lead to or who you may meet in the process.

Mahatma Gandhi said it best, "The best way to find yourself is to lose yourself in the service of others." A major element of your career transition journey is "finding yourself" and learning and discovering more about who you want to be in the next chapter of your career. That discovery will come in many forms, but it will also come in serving and helping others while you simultaneously seek assistance and support from your network. Serving others will also contribute not only to your "favor bank" which we feature earlier in this book, but more importantly, it will contribute to helping you maintain a positive attitude, perspective, and mindset.

REMIND YOURSELF WHAT YOUR PASSIONS WERE WHEN YOU STARTED YOUR CAREER

"If you are lucky enough to find something that you love, and you have a shot at being good at it, don' stop, don't put it down."

–Taylor Swift

As you journey through your career transition, take some quality time to remind yourself what your passions were when you launched your career – sports, travel, fashion, fitness, music, food, non-profits, etc. In other words, remind yourself what type of work you loved then and what passions have surfaced in the past few years. No one every dictated or legislated that you had to settle for a job that you disliked. If you take time to remind yourself of past and present passions, you might want to pursue that as one of the paths in your current job search. Your search does not have to be exclusively linked to your most recent job or solely to a certain industry. In a column titled, "6 Fresh Ways To Find Your Passion," Corrina Gordon-Barnes writes, "The path of passion is where you do things that scare you enough, without leaving you in a constant state of fear. Expand your comfort zone, rather than leaving it." So, get out of your comfort zone and scare yourself a bit. There is no better time than the present to immerse yourself in your passions, experiment and explore a variety of opportunities that could result in you starting to write the next chapter in your career.

Gordon-Barnes, C. (2022, June 22). *6 Steps That'll Help You Find Your Passion*. The Muse. https://www.themuse.com/advice/6-fresh-ways-to-find-your-passion

TAKE ADVANTAGE OF A T LETTER

*"When love and skill work together,
expect a masterpiece."*

–John Ruskin

Creating and leveraging a T Letter in your job search is a critical artifact that will greatly enhance your probability of success in not only obtaining interviews but can also be the difference in your being selected over the other candidates to fill the position.

The best part of a T Letter is how easy it is to create one:

Step 1 – Split the paper down the middle lengthwise

Step 2 – Take a printed copy of the job requirements and highlight all the items the employer is seeking and list them down the left side of the page

Step 3 – On the right side of the page, next to each job requirement, list your experience, skills and/or education you have that demonstrate that you meet the requirement

This T Letter document is gold as it basically makes the case that you are qualified for the job that you have initiated your candidacy for. Add a paragraph on top and at the bottom and you now have a great cover letter. Whether this goes to a gatekeeper in human resources or the hiring manager themselves, they can now clearly and effectively see that you are a candidate that meets the job requirements they seek and your probability for being selected to come in and interview for the position has increased substantially. Another great thing to do is bring a copy of your T Letter to your interview as a leave behind for the hiring manager. Think of it this way - everyone who was invited to interview should meet the requirements for the position. However, you just provided the hiring manager with a well-thought through list of why you are an exact match for the position. If the hiring manager simply "reuses" this as their justification to their boss as to why you were selected, you just provided your candidacy another edge over the other finalists.

PRACTICE PARS

"Obstacles don't have to stop you. If you run into a wall, don't turn around and give up. Figure out how to climb it, go through it, or work around it."

–Michael Jordan

Creating and effectively leveraging Problem/Action/Result (PARs) are critical to multiple steps throughout your job search process. Let's explore why and how they are important to your candidacy. The master version of your resume should contain many PARs that cover all the experience related to your responsibilities of the various positions that you have held. You can then pick and choose from this master list of PARs when you are applying to a position by selecting those that are applicable to the position that you are applying to. Considering the specific position that you are applying, you may want to reword or clarify certain aspects so that information that pertains to the opportunity is very clear and easily understood. The PAR, if used correctly, should also serve as the basis for your answers during the interview. This allows you to explain how you encountered similar challenges in your career previously, how you were able to meet and overcome these challenges, and the benefit and results you were able to realize for your employer and their clients. Please remember that when you are sharing this information with the interviewer be very aware of any verbal signs or body language they are providing. Also, be clear to delineate if the accomplishment was yours personally or if you worked as part of a team or led the team to achieve them. If they seem to be losing interest, wrap-up the answer or ask the interviewer if you can further explain a specific aspect of the question that they posed. Always have some well thought through questions for the interviewer in advance so you can use these to find out more about the position and the employer that may not have been covered in the job description and any other information that you were provided.

DEVELOP A POINT SYSTEM
TO MEASURE YOUR PROSPECTING

*"Real success comes in small portions day by day. You
need to take pleasure in life's daily little treasures. It is
the most important in measuring success."*

–Denis Waitley

As you go through your job search transition, you need a way
in which to gauge your level of effort and success. Many
will look at whether they have obtained a job offer as the key
to whether their job search is successful or not. Achieving a
job offer is the ultimate objective of your effort, but if you
have that as your only measure of success it will lead to a long
process and contribute to the many ups and downs you will
face. So, what we suggest instead is to look at all the activities
that you must perform during a job search which includes, but
are not limited to:

- Adding new contacts to your network
- Identifying and attending networking meetings

- Identifying and establishing relationships with recruiters
- Creating and honing your resume
- Developing PARS (Problem, Action, Result) statements for your resume and interviewing
- Honing your interviewing skills and preparing for interviews
- Researching and identifying strong potential employers to target
- Identifying and networking with individuals who work currently at, previously worked at, or can introduce you to individual(s) that work at your targeted employers
- Making qualified submissions (making a case with your resume and T-Letter) for jobs you are strong match
- Turning unknown to known opportunities
- Going on interviews
- Following up after interviews with thank you letters

Now, assign a point value to each of these activities and then dig down and set an objective that if you work really hard and smart, how many points you can realistically expect to achieve on a weekly basis. Track your progress and how many points you accumulate each week and if you hit your target, celebrate and reward yourself in some way. Maybe you would like to see a movie, maybe you enjoy reading a good book, but do something for yourself that recognizes the hard work and that you accomplished your goals for that week. Also, if you have a significant other, share with them your goals, activities, and accomplishments so they can understand all the work you are putting in. Communication with a significant other and family during a job search is essential as in the end, you are all affected by the outcome.

TURN UNKNOWN INTO KNOWN OPPORTUNITIES

*"There are things known and things unknown
and in between are doors."*

–Jim Morrison

How does one go about seeing a job posted and then turn this opportunity that you have found from an unknown to a known opportunity? Thankfully social media exists and is critical in helping us with this task as we now have a great resource like LinkedIn which allow us to operationalize and leverage the six degrees of separation. So, to begin with, we need to know the name of the firm that the job opportunity is for. Then, using LinkedIn as an example, here is a scenario you can follow to achieve it.

1. Go to LinkedIn and see who you are connected to at the firm who posted the job:

a. If you have a 1st level connection at the firm, you should go through and make your case for your candidacy by doing a qualified submission.

   i. Produce a T-Letter as part of your cover letter

   ii. Make the case with your resume for your candidacy for the position

b. Reach out to your connection and request time to speak with them and explain you are seeking to learn more about the firm/employer.

c. During the discussion ask questions about the culture, what levels exist and how they work as well as related pay structures. You may be lucky enough that your contact can even explain the group in which the job is within and the hiring manager. Then share the specific opportunity you are interested in and share the case as to why you feel you would be a strong match.

2. If you don't have a level 1 connection at the targeted firm, you can:

a. See if you have a level 2 connection that can in-turn request that they make an introduction for you to someone at the firm.

b. Leverage your network on LinkedIn, Facebook, and other channels to network your way into the firm to simply have discussions and learn more about firms you are targeting and to establish contacts at these targeted firms. Send a brief email to the networking groups members that you are targeting XYZ firm as a potential employer and would appreciate if anyone who works there, previously worked there, or knows someone there can make an introduction for you.

MANAGE MULTIPLE OPPORTUNITIES

*"Most people miss great opportunities because
of their misperception of time. Don't wait!
The time will never be just right."*

–Stephen C. Hogan

A great problem for anyone in a job search is to have too many opportunities but you must be careful to maximize your reach but not beyond your ability to effectively manage the universe of opportunities you have and are actively working. As previously suggested, carefully keep opportunity related details in a spreadsheet that you constantly update and mine the sheet, so you understand when your interviews are, what follow-ups you committed to and when they are to be done. It is critical that you effectively manage all these contacts, opportunities, and interactions during your job search as again you are leaving a lasting impression with each interaction. Missing returning a call on a specific day and the time that you committed to getting the date and time of an interview wrong will negate all the time and work you invested in identifying and securing those opportunities, so you want to ensure you make the most of each opportunity and are fully prepared to do so. Also, share your progress and your tracking sheet with those you are close to - parents, spouse, significant other, children. You need to realize that they are going through your job search with you. It's critical to share and communicate what you are going through as they may be able to provide good advice or suggestions for improvement. They can share in your gains and help pull you through the challenging times.

FIT THE CULTURE

*"Company culture is the backbone of
any successful organization."*

–Gary Vaynerchuk

Once a potential employer has decided on you as a candidate and an interview has been set, the major factor in determining who gets selected to fill the opportunity from the slate of candidates is the one who is the best cultural fit. It is critical that you really pull out all your stops in networking to turn this unknown into a known opportunity. You need to identify someone who currently works or previously worked at the targeted firm so that they can explain to you more about the firm, its' values, history, unwritten rules, vision and culture. Ideally, you would have liked to have gone through all of this when you were going through your process of researching your targets to prospect, but the possibility exists a job opportunity may present itself that looks good but isn't with one of your targeted firms. Then, you must kick your primary research into high gear to accomplish your diligence on the firm quickly. The best way to do so is through your network. If you don't have someone who is a direct contact currently working at this potential future employer, try to use a mutual contact to gain an introduction to an individual on the inside who can schedule a conversation. Another alternative is to send a purposely short email to your network requesting if anyone currently works or had previously worked at the employer that you are targeting or knows of someone that is there and simply ask that they contact you directly. Once you have qualified this contact you can then work with them one-on-one.

PLAY BY THE
PROSPECTING RULES

*"Active prospecting let's people know they matter;
that you've sought them out."*

–Diane Helbig

There are many guidelines that you need to be aware of and follow which are not documented anywhere related to a specific job search that can have a critical impact on you getting the job you are pursuing.

Rule 1 – Once you apply to a position through a recruiter, you are now locked into association with that recruiter at the targeted firm for a certain period of time (usually six months). So, if you find another opportunity that interests you at that same firm, unless you go through the same recruiter it may disqualify your candidacy and doing so may extend the timeframe you are now locked into that recruiter at that firm.

Rule 2 – If you are using a recruiter at a targeted firm, run everything through them as they are your partner in the opportunity. If you go around them without their knowledge it could have negative consequences on your candidacy

Rule 3 – Always tell the truth and don't embellish or fabricate experience, skills or competencies as even if you land the position you won't be able to meet the requirements of your responsibilities.

Rule 4 – Never stop networking. Once you land, continue growing your network among both those in your new firm but also keep your personal network alive and growing as well. You never know when a transition could come again.

Rule 5 – Give to those you are networking with to the greatest extent possible as it will come back to you many times over.

Rule 6 – Your job search will be the hardest job you ever have so it's critical you remain focused, keep up your regular qualified submissions, and follow-through on known submissions whenever able, and work to set aggressive, but attainable objectives weekly.

Rule 7 – If you share your resume with a recruiter, be very specific that they aren't to share with a prospective employer without your knowledge and consent.

Rule 8 – Think out-of-the-box and be innovative and creative in prospecting your targets and ensure they have positions consistent with your passion.

Rule 9 – One of the hardest things is to deal with is the uncertainty, but don't let the uncertainty cause you to take actions that aren't consistent with the best practices we shared as they will have a good chance of extending your time in search.

GAIN THE EDGE OVER OTHER CANDIDATES

"You've got to keep reinventing. You'll have new competitors."

–Ginni Rometty

Throughout these lessons, there are numerous items all meant to give your candidacy an edge throughout the job search process. Each individual item only gives you a slight edge, but when they are combined together, they give your candidacy a significant edge in aggregate. This is intended to recap those items that will give you an edge and when they all converge, give your candidacy a significant edge over the other candidates being considered:

Making the case with your resume – makes it easier to see you as a match for the opportunity and increases your chance of gaining an interview.

<u>Turning an unknown to a known opportunity</u> – getting a recommendation or introduction directly into the hiring manager is the holy grail for helping a job seekers candidacy. Achieving this will substantially increase the probability of success.

<u>PARs</u> – this is the basis for your conversations during the interview and provides tangible evidence you've been there and tackled the challenge and can deliver measurable value.

<u>T Letter</u> – methodically shows that you meet all the published requirements for the position and provides the hiring manager with the justification of why you were hired that they can in turn use with their manager to justify hiring you.

<u>Effectively leveraging a recruiter in your search</u> – know the do's and don'ts and find out which recruiters are used by your targeted company. Often, a potential employer has a limited approved list of recruiters that they will work with who are on their approved vendor list. Understanding this may be the critical piece of information to help you gain access to the recruiter that you are targeting.

<u>Networking Impactfully</u> – build and strengthen your network with every interaction. Never stop networking even after landing both at your new employer and outside of work. Remember the strength and reach of your network is the only rainy-day insurance policy your career will ever have.

INCREASE YOUR INTERVIEW SELECTION CHANCES

"When it comes to luck, you make your own."

–Bruce Springsteen

You need to leverage these critical elements in unison to increase your probability of being selected from hundreds possibly thousands of other candidates just to be interviewed:

- Build a strong and extensive network that you can leverage through turning an unknown to known opportunity as well as increasing the amount of people who know of you and know of your value proposition which may lead to uncovering unknown jobs and help in identifying and tapping the hidden job market.

- Make the case for your candidacy with your resume providing all the information clearly so that the critical gatekeepers see you as a strong match for the open position.

- Carefully craft PARs on your resume that demonstrates your competency to meet the requirements of the position listed in the job description.

- Use a T Letter effectively as part of your strategic approach to writing and submitting a cover letter.

- Transform this unknown opportunity into a known opportunity.

- Get someone to deliver a reference and recommendation by phone, email or in-person to the hiring manager. Prepare any reference in advance by sharing the job description of the position you are pursuing. Also, share the resume and your cover letter including the T Letter. If you prepare your reference thoroughly, they will be able to speak much better when providing your recommendation. Additionally, keep those providing references apprised. Did you get the opportunity? Are there other opportunities you may need them to serve as a reference for?

- If a recruiter is involved, have them present you as the preferred candidate.

RETHINK RELOCATION

"Remember to enjoy the freedom of being able to work from anywhere and the flexibility to adapt your work to your life rather than the other way around."

–Alex Muench

If you are considering taking a position that requires relocation and/or relocation is your priority and finding a job in the city you are planning on relocating to, there are many variables that you need to consider and research to ensure you are making an informed decision and have all the needed information in order to do so effectively. Learn if you have a family member or someone in your network in the target location who can provide insight to the many questions you may have regarding the new geography that you are considering moving to. In addition to the direct questions such as home prices, property taxes, state taxes, and the commuting situation, think of all the indirect considerations such as the quality of doctors in the immediate area, proximity to hospital(s), school systems and other considerations that may be important to you. Research and learn if there are job search and networking groups in the area you are targeting and start getting involved with them, even if you can only do so remotely, so you can get many perspectives on the area that you are considering. There are countless resources that you can leverage to help gather the information you need regarding the area that you are considering relocating to. It's critical you gain as much insight into relocation as possible so that you can make the best-informed decision.

PRIORITIZE THE NEED
FOR THE SPEED OF TRUST

"Trust is built with consistency."

–Lincoln Chafee

The reason connections are so important in job search is that the connection's level of strength of relationship with the contact you are targeting can be a significant asset to your search. If you think back to most of the jobs you have had, many, if not all, were secured through networking. Networking is essential to your job search in several ways as we share throughout this book. It is critical for turning an unknown into a known opportunity, for getting a recommendation to the hiring manager, but to us, most importantly it unlocks the unknown job market. Managers may not have a job requisition created for every position that they have budgeted and/ or may have discretion into how they meet the demand. Thus, when you are networking, and someone trusted by a hiring manager introduces you they are now meeting you in a different light. It isn't to measure how you fit with a job requisition. It is listening to the value you bring and the needs that they have. That is the unknown job market. So, if the hiring manager establishes a connection with you and they have a need, don't be surprised if you find yourself in an informal interview without a job requisition. The great thing about this is that if the recruiter really wants to hire you, they may not even post the job and consider other candidates. These are two more reasons why having targeted companies and networking impactfully are so critical to the success of your job search.

IDENTIFY THE
HIDDEN JOB MARKET

"In today's fast-paced job market, some of the most exciting opportunities remain hidden from job boards and online listings."

–Mariam Gogidze

You may have heard in life that, "it's not important what you know, but it's more important who you know." After many years of spearheading one of the nation's leading job search and networking groups, The Breakfast Club NJ, Frank Kovacs has heard this old saying evolve to "It's important who knows you." This is the crux of successfully unlocking the hidden job market. Throughout this book, we detail the critical importance of the following:

- Treating every interaction as an interview
- Always networking – "always be connecting"

It is critically important to consistently focus on expanding the number of people in your network – especially "who knows you" and your value proposition and brand. You can enlist the help of your entire network if you interact with them appropriately and build solid relationships so that they will be out there and ready to mobilize when opportunities arise consistent with your competency and they will recommend and/or consider you. Ultimately, you want to evolve your network to the point where the hiring manager "knows you" and is interested in you and the value that you can deliver. That is the brilliance that is in identifying the hidden job market.

Gogidze, M. (2023, September 7). *Hidden Job Market Is Real*. LinkedIn. https://www.linkedin.com/pulse/hidden-job-market-real-mariam-gogidze/?utm_source=rss&utm_campaign=articles_sitemaps&utm_medium=google_news

AVOID THE COMPENSATION CONVERSATION

"I don't talk about my salary."

–Howard Stern

We have all been there where we are just having the initial discussion regarding a position and either the recruiter or even the hiring manager may be asking us what are your salary requirements? Now you were having a great conversation and don't want to potentially derail this by discussing compensation too early and possibly kill your candidacy. The good news is that compensation has become so complex in today's environment that by answering this question as follows should provide you the latitude you need to avoid having it prematurely and delaying it to a time where it would be more appropriate.

We have had recruiters address the networking group and their suggestion has been to ask the potential employer's representative what the position was budgeted for and once they share, tell them if your salary requirements are within the range.

We prefer a slightly different tact where you explain to the employer representative that compensation has changed so significantly where salary is just one component and the proposed benefits and their costs are important in determining the salary needed. For example, is health coverage included or does the employee pay part and if so what percent and amount? This simple point can significantly sway total compensation as well as compensation elements such as if the company has a pension, if not 401K, and if so, what is the 401K match percent? Many times we have found the employer's representative sympathetic and they will then explain some of these details or the range for the job to see if it's in the ballpark.

Whichever approach you take, ensure that you provide the minimum information required as you don't want to negotiate until you have them convinced that you are the candidate they want. One final piece of advice, try to negotiate all the finer points with HR rather than with the hiring manager. Once you start working, you will need to work closely with the hiring manager, and you don't want anything to disrupt the relationship that you are forming.

MANAGING MULTIPLE OFFERS

*"Chase after the dream, don't chase
after the money."*

–Old Dominion

What a great problem to have – consider yourself blessed instead of looking at this as a quandary. At the beginning of your search, you want to make a list of attributes that you want to consider in the ideal position then rank and order them in priority and importance from most to least:

- Length of commute
- Salary of position
- Benefits that employer offers
- Where position is located
- Industry outlook for potential employer and its ranking in the industry
- Opportunity for advancement beyond current position
- Quality of work/life balance

- Nature of responsibilities
- Ability to work remotely
- Amount of vacation and PTO days
- Long term outlook of employer, industry
- Culture of organization

Then, once you have your multiple offers go back to this original list as it will remind you what you were seeking and what you considered important. Use this as the basis for comparing the different offers you received and to help in making a decision between them.

LEARN TO NEGOTIATE

"Let us never negotiate out of fear. But let us never fear to negotiate."

–John F. Kennedy

Negotiation is a skill that can be used in many different areas of our lives such as business, personal relationships, and everyday interactions. Becoming a master negotiator can get you what you want more often than you realize while building stronger relationships, as well as resolving conflicts much more easily. But being aware of our past experiences in negotiations can prevent us from engaging in negotiations. Leave those past experiences exactly where they are, in the past! Vanessa Van Edwards said it best, "If you believe you can be a better negotiator, you are more likely to become a better negotiator." You can achieve anything you put your mind to, but you have to believe it in your heart and soul first. Here are a few key tips on how to negotiate effectively:

Do your research – Before entering negotiations, make sure to research and understand the company's needs and interests.

Knowing key information will help you position yourself better to make more strategic and informed decisions.

- Be prepared to walk away – You are not tied down to one place or organization, so it is important to remember the opportunity as well as the value you bring to the table. This could leverage and make organizations more likely to compromise.

- Be assertive, but not aggressive- Confidence is key in this situation. Standing up for your interest is important but be sure to be respectful of the company's limits and capacity as well. You can always find common ground with proper communication.

- Practice active listening – Sure, you have heard how important it is to be an active listener, but do you put it into practice? One of the most effective ways to build trust and rapport is to listen actively. Pay attention to what is being said, ask clarifying questions, and don't forget to summarize key points to show that you were 100% focused on everything being discussed.

- Be creative – Throughout this book, you should have already been thinking of creative ways to approach winning the job but make sure you keep the creative juices flowing when it comes to negotiations. Thinking outside of the box and coming up with solutions that meet the needs of both sides is the goal. Work towards that and you will come out better than expected.

- Be patient – This might be the most important and most challenging part of negotiations. This part takes the most time, especially because important agreements and decisions may not happen overnight. Remember to be patient and trust the process because eventually with time, both sides need to be happy with the final offer/decision.

Becoming a great negotiator will not be a skill that is developed overnight. It will take much practice, and at first, many uncomfortable conversations, but with time, your confidence will grow, and you will be on your way to becoming a master at negotiating the things you need in your life that will bring ultimate happiness.

Van Edwards, V. (n.d.). *How to Negotiate (With 12 Science-Backed Strategies to Win)*. Science Of People. https://www.scienceofpeople.com/negotiation/

PART V

Make Major Advances With Marketing, Research And Preparation

SUPERSIZE YOUR SKILLS
ON LINKEDIN

"A winner is someone who recognizes his God-given talents, works his tail off to develop the into skills, and uses these skills to accomplish his goals."

–Larry Bird

The skills you carefully select to display on your LinkedIn profile and getting the endorsement of those skills and even how your order these on your LinkedIn profile are critical to the success of your candidacy. First, it is suggested that you pull approximately a dozen position descriptions for jobs you are interested in pursuing. The reason is to identify the top skills that the employers of these jobs are seeking. Then, if you possess these skills make sure that they are among those skills listed on your LinkedIn profile and work to get them endorsed. The best way to do so is to go to the profiles of current and/or former colleagues and others in your network and endorse their skills. Most times they will want to return the favor and will, in turn endorse your skills. You want to order your skills for different purposes at different times. Only the first three skills display in the default view of your LinkedIn profile. So, if you are a job seeker you want the top three you have seen on the job requirements and/or those that support your brand the best. If you are in process of looking for endorsements, you may want to put those you are most seeking endorsement for on top as those seeking to endorse you will usually endorse those skills that are easiest to access. Finally those skills that will label you as legacy even if well endorsed may be causing your brand more harm than good and if this is the case even if they are heavily endorsed it may be more in your interest to delete them then to keep them on your profile and potentially keeping you from securing the job you seek. This same logic applies to when you are doing a qualified submission. You want to include that information that "makes the case for your candidacy." If it isn't relevant to that point it becomes a detractor to the hiring manager and could work negatively for your candidacy.

MASTER SOFT & HARD SKILLS

"Hard skills get you in, soft skills get you far."

–Sahil Lavingia

The industry is in a perpetual state of evolution, with changes spanning technology, company culture, and even the way we work, whether in physical offices or remotely. Amidst this evolution, the rise of A.I. has spotlighted certain skills as more crucial than ever before. Hard and soft skills will always be something you hear when discussions of career growth and professional development are at play, but when we focus on the bigger picture, both sets of skills can make you valuable in personal and professional spaces. Career and personal life are intertwined whether we like to believe it or not. To be most effective, let's focus on winning the job and utilizing the resources of your resume to do it. The skills that employers are looking for are listed right on the job description, and this is where your analytical and awareness skills come into play. In the Career Guide section of Indeed, Jamie Birt stated, "Hard and soft skills that employers want to see might be found in the "requirements," "education" or "desired skills" sections of the post." Being able to find these skills will give you a significant advantage over the competition.

First and foremost, digital and data analysis skills should top your list. Proficiency with computers, software, and online platforms is indispensable for productivity and staying connected in this fast-paced environment. Equally vital are problem-solving, adaptability, and critical thinking skills, given the industry's relentless pace of transformation. These skills empower professionals to navigate the ever-shifting landscape with finesse. In addition, collaboration and creativity are pivotal when functioning within a team, as we all recognize that a cohesive team is fundamental to an organization's success. Lastly, but by no means least, communication and leadership skills are non-negotiable. In this unprecedented era, individuals with strong leadership and communication abilities are at the forefront of innovation and revenue generation. Moreover, they infuse the workplace with a sense of enjoyment and purpose.

Birt, J. (2023, September 7). *Hard Skills vs. Soft Skills: What's the Difference?* Indeed. https://www.indeed.com/career-advice/resumes-cover-letters/hard-skills-vs-soft-skills

BECOME AN EQ EXPERT

"The most important decision you make is to be in a good mood."

–Voltaire

Emotional intelligence (EQ) is a critical skill for achieving success in any career, and it has become even more essential in the post-COVID world. EQ involves the ability to understand and manage not only your own emotions but also those of others. Now if this is a new term to you, that's OK. Most professionals in the industry are learning this for the first time as well. Remember, companies are evolving and constantly working to become more inclusive, allocating large sums of money to make sure it's being done right. When discussing coaching interventions and growth strategies, Tomas Chamarro-Premuzic wrote in *Harvard Business Review*, "The underlying reasoning is that, whereas IQ is very hard to change, EQ can increase with deliberate practice and training." Simply put, with proper reinforcement and awareness, your EQ can grow far beyond what you believe capable.

In the current industry landscape, there are several compelling reasons why EQ is paramount for career success. Firstly, the recent COVID-19 pandemic has ushered in a period of significant uncertainty and change in workplaces worldwide. Individuals with high EQ excel at adapting to these changes, remaining composed and productive even in challenging situations. Strong relationships have always been crucial in professional settings, but they have taken on increased significance in the current industry. Those with high EQ are adept at building and sustaining positive relationships with colleagues, clients, and customers.

Conflicts are an inherent part of any workplace in the current industry, but high EQ individuals have a distinct advantage when it comes to resolving conflicts constructively. They possess the ability to listen to others' perspectives, maintain composure under pressure, and find mutually beneficial solutions. Effective leadership is another arena where emotional intelligence shines in the current industry. Leaders with high EQ skills can motivate and inspire their team members, foster trust, and create a positive work environment, which is especially valuable in these evolving times. Stress management is also crucial, given the pervasive sense of uncertainty and pressure. Individuals with high EQ skills are better equipped to manage stress effectively, ensuring they remain productive and resilient.

Numerous resources such as books, articles, and online courses, are available to assist you in your endeavor to increase your EQ. Seeking feedback from colleagues and mentors can also prove to be a great avenue. In practical terms, improving your emotional intelligence involves several actionable steps. Begin by cultivating self-awareness—recognize your emotions and identify what triggers them. Subsequently, work on emotion control, which entails managing your emotions and expressing them appropriately. Empathy is another crucial facet of EQ, as it enables you to comprehend and share the feelings of others, fostering stronger relationships and conflict-resolution skills. Effective communication of your emotions is essential, as it can significantly impact your relationships and career trajectory. Lastly, maintaining a positive and optimistic attitude can be a powerful asset in the workplace, enhancing productivity, creativity, and resilience.

While developing your emotional intelligence may require time and effort, it is a valuable investment in your professional and personal growth, paving the way for greater success and fulfillment in your career and life.

Chamorro-Premuzic, T. (2013, May 29). *Can You Really Improve Your Emotional Intelligence?*. Harvard Business Review. https://hbr.org/2013/05/can-you-really-improve-your-em

NETWORK WITH IMPACT

"The successful networkers I know, the ones receiving tons of referrals and feeling truly happy about themselves, continually put the other person's needs ahead of their own."

–Bob Burg

When you are networking, it is critical that you are proactively networking and you don't just obtain contact information from the person you are networking with, but truly establish a relationship with them. Don't be the person who goes to a networking event and just looks to collect the most business cards from others. You have to begin by being willing to help the other individual you are networking with openly with no expectation of reciprocation. Think of it as every relationship has an emotional bank account and you are creating this account with someone and contributing to it. Then, when you have a need, you will have many in your network who will be willing to help you in return. It is critical that you treat each interaction as an "interview." Remember to brand yourself and establish a good impression with the individual you are networking with. Keith Ferrazzi's *Never Eat Alone* or Dale Carnegie's *How To Win Friends And Influence People* offer very sound advice for how to properly interact when networking. Ensure you get the individual's business card so that you have their contact information. Following the event, make sure you follow up with the individual and extend an invitation for them to connect with you on LinkedIn, hopefully scheduling either a phone call or possibly meet over coffee, but work towards evolving the new contact into a relationship.

HIGHLIGHT YOUR IMPACT

*"A life is not important except in the impact
it has on other lives."*

–Jackie Robinson

Becoming an impactful team player is a fundamental requirement for success within any organization. This involves surpassing the boundaries of your job description, actively contributing to your team's accomplishments, and fostering a positive transformation within your company. When young professionals come looking for guidance, it is always communicated to remember that it's not where you start, but it's about where you finish. When looking for your first job out of college, or you are switching industries, have an open mind. Be open to the jobs that you are not good at, but great at! Doing so will help you reach certain goals and build your highlight reel. Stacey Phillips says it best, stating, "Always deliver high-quality work and make sure others know they can trust you to get the job done." Effectively highlighting these impacts is essential, and you can achieve this by quantifying your results, such as increasing sales by 10% or reducing turnover through initiatives like hosting happy hours and weekly cross-departmental meetings. The key lies in being specific about your contributions and maintaining a positive and enthusiastic attitude throughout your journey.

It's imperative to keep a record of your noteworthy achievements, regardless of their size. This practice helps you recall your accomplishments and allows you to spotlight them when the need arises. Regular one-on-one meetings with your manager, along with discussions with influential figures in your career, including mentors and sponsors, are invaluable. Monthly, semi-annual, and annual check-ins and reviews offer excellent opportunities to showcase your impact. During these sessions, you can not only discuss your achievements but also set goals and pinpoint areas for improvement. Constructive feedback is an indispensable tool for personal and professional development. It aids in recognizing your strengths and addressing your weaknesses. Embrace feedback with an open mind and leverage it to enhance your performance.

By consistently highlighting your impact, documenting your successes, and actively participating in performance reviews, you can effectively demonstrate your value to your company, positioning yourself for long-term success. Being open to and applying constructive feedback can be just as valuable. Take the initiative to proactively share your achievements with leaders and colleagues; don't wait for someone to ask. When requesting feedback, ensure your communication is clear and concise. Maintain a positive demeanor even when addressing areas that require improvement and remain humble throughout your journey. By adhering to these principles, you can effectively showcase your impact and cultivate a prosperous and enduring career.

Phillips, S. (n.d.). *10 Of The Best Ways To Make An Impact At Work*. I Connect Engineers. https://iconnectengineers.com/blog/10-of-the-best-ways-to-make-an-impact-at-work/

SCRIPT YOUR STORYTELLING

"I'm obsessed with giving the audience something they don't see coming."

–Jordan Peele

Even if you are an accountant, engineer, or a web designer, you need to specialize in storytelling when you are in the midst of a career transition. The individual who can tell their story in the most compelling and engaging manner will win the job. In June 2018, Karl Smart and Jerry DiMaria of Central Michigan University published a scholarly journal article titled, "Using Storytelling As A Job Search Strategy." In their abstract, they write, "This article demonstrates and reinforces the role that well-told stories play in the success of the job-search process. Building on narrative theory, impression management, and an increased use of behavioral-based questions in interviews, well-crafted stories about work and educational experiences demonstrate skills applicants possess and convey them to interviewers in memorable ways." Take quality time well before a cup-of-coffee conversation, formal interview or group networking meeting to script your story. While the core elements of your script - your education, experience and successes - will stay the same, there will be times where you will need to deliver them in seconds in the form of an elevator pitch and other times over the course of an all-day interview to various decision makers. Your success in scripting your story will come in the sequence in which you tell your story and how effectively you integrate anecdotes and past successes that are most relevant to your audience. "An important part of storytelling is being able to confidently share your story about why you left your last job," commented Keith Green, a seasoned public relations and marketing communication professional. "Get it down and practice it just like your elevator speech. If you were laid off, there was a restructuring or ownership change that led to your departure, share it and move on. You will find that people are almost always sympathetic and a surprising number of them were in your shoes and can relate. The truth is, people won't care about the details and will want to focus on helping you." Success will also come in your delivery of your story - confident, articulate and engaging. From this day forward on your journey to the next opportunity in your career, transform yourself into the world's greatest storyteller. After all, you know the subject matter, your background and experience, better than anyone.

DiMaria, J., & Smart, K. L. (2018, June). *Use Storytelling As A Job Search Strategy*. Sage Journals. https://journals.sagepub.com/doi/abs/10.11 77/2329490618769877?journalCode=bcqe

KNOW 10 TOPICS YOU
CAN DISCUSS FOR 10 MINUTES

"I'm definitely a people person. I love socializing and being around people and having a good conversation.

–Emily Deschanel

Whether at work, a networking event, or a social function, you will want to master the art of conducting conversations. There are some who believe that in today's social media society conducting a face-to-face conversation is a lost art, which makes it even more impressive when a job candidate can look in the eye of the person they are conversing with and engage in discuss a wide variety of topics from pop culture to politics and sports to society. Longtime public relations practitioner David Siroty is a big believer in thoroughly knowing 10 topics across various segments – sports, pop culture, politics, music, movies, food, movies, business - that you can discuss for 10 minutes each. It's what makes Dave one of those people at a function that others tend to gravitate towards. He has the ability to carry on a conversation with anyone across a variety of topics. If your 10 topics are your secret weapon, you can pivot and transition off any conversation that you walk into and turn the table so that the conversation is now centered on your areas of expertise. Applying this lesson also extends your ability to converse with a diverse number of individuals no matter age, gender, or background. Throughout your career, you don't want to become a wallflower or be placed in the shy box. Master the 10 topics in 10 minutes lesson and you will always be at the center of the conversation.

DEVELOP YOUR UNIQUE PERSONAL VALUE PROPOSITION

*"Cultivating your value proposition in life is the way
to move forward. You are the raw material
of your own destiny."*

–Bryant H. McGill

In an article *Harvard Business Review* article, Bill Barnett clearly communicates the importance for job seekers in developing their value proposition. "Your personal value proposition (PVP) is at the heart of your career strategy. It's the foundation for everything in a job search and career progression — targeting potential employers, attracting the help of others, and explaining why you're the one to pick. It's why to hire you, not someone else." What is something so unique about you that very few people can ever claim? What is something you accomplished at school or work which is one-of-a-kind? What is your talent or skill or hobby that will set you apart from every other candidate applying for the same job? As you pursue the next opportunity in your career, you want to contemplate and consider your unique personal value proposition that is not only unique but communicates that it will deliver value to your future employer. Brands go through this exercise regularly as they market and advertise in an attempt to win over customers from the competition. For Domino's, for many years, it was that they would deliver your pizza in less than 30 minutes guaranteed. Duolingo makes learning a new language fun. With those examples in mind, begin to ideate and construct your unique value proposition. It is not only something that you will you be able to articulate in your elevator pitch or formal interview, but it could also find its way onto your resume if you can write it in a pithy way that really pops in a relevant and meaningful way.

Barnett, B. (2011, November 17). *Build Your Personal Value Proposition.* Harvard Business Review . https://hbr.org/2011/11/a-value-propo sition-for-your-c

PREPARE YOUR POSITIONING STATEMENT

"Focus on identifying your target audience, communicating an authentic message that they want and need and project yourself as an 'expert' within your niche."

–Kim Garst

What does your personal and professional brand stand for? How can you deliver value to an organization? What makes you different than every other candidate that is interviewing for the exact same job? Just as a brand will develop a positioning statement to effectively communicate how their service or product fills a consumer need that the competition does not, you need to do the same. Take a step back and pause as you are racing ahead to your next job interview. After carefully reviewing the roles, responsibilities and metrics for success, if the employer provides them, start to write and develop your brand positioning statement. Like a consumer brand, debate and determine how your experience, skills and service will effectively fill a need at this potential employer that no other candidate can fill the way you can. The candidate that can develop and deliver that type of compelling position in their interview will differentiate themselves from the other finalists and improve their probability of being selected to fill the position.

BUILD OUT
YOUR BRAND NARRATIVE

*"An authentic and honest brand narrative
is fundamental today; otherwise,
you will simply be edited out."*

–Marco Bizzarri

"The best marketers are storytellers. After all, how many customers truly make purchasing decisions based on statistics or a cost-benefit analysis? Emotional appeals are the truest way to connect with customers, and stories are the most powerful method for doing so. This is what makes your brand's narrative so important." Like brands who market to consumers, you will need to develop your brand narrative. Most individuals who are competing for job opportunities don't consider themselves brands, but they are, and they need to market themselves like consumer brands. The way to do that is by developing your brand narrative. It consists of your history and your experience. It should pay homage to your upbringing and your values. It should also be forward-looking as well and offer a glimpse into your vision for innovation and transformation. It can include your unique value proposition and perhaps even your elevator pitch. You should take quality time to outline it at first and then write it out. While you most likely will never need to submit it in written form, every element of your brand narrative will be used as you participate in the interview process. There are no rules in developing your personal brand narrative, but by investing quality time in contemplating it and writing it, you will automatically, without even knowing it, start to develop the storytelling that you will deliver in a compelling and engaging manner when you conduct formal and informal interviews. With each interview, you will refine and evolve your narrative and one day, it will deliver the next opportunity in your career to you.

Bee, H. (2018, August 17). *The Power Of Brand Narrative: 5 Ways To Create It*. Chief Marketer. https://www.chiefmarketer.com/the-power-of-brand-narrative-5-ways-to-create-it/

PERFECT YOUR ELEVATOR PITCH

*"The purpose of an elevator pitch is to describe
a situation or solution so compelling that the person
you're with wants to hear more even after
the elevator ride is over."*

–Seth Godin

For *Forbes*, Nancy Collamer succinctly explains why every individual in the midst of a career transition needs to perfect their elevator pitch well before they ever get on the elevator... or attend a cocktail party of some other function. "If you're looking for a job, one of the first tasks on your to-do list should be crafting an ideal 'elevator pitch.' It's the 30-second speech that summarizes who you are, what you do and why you'd be a perfect candidate. You should be able to reel off your elevator pitch at any time, from a job interview to a cocktail party conversation with someone who might be able to help you land a position." You are not always going to have the opportunity to explain and detail your life's work. In fact, there are many times where you will have less than a minute to impress someone enough into investing more time in you. This is where your elevator pitch comes in. Typically, at the conclusion of career support group meetings, everyone in attendance has 15-20 seconds to introduce themselves via their elevator pitch. The most compelling pitches are always the ones that are unique, different, engaging, clever and usually get a few laughs, while still delivering a clear and concise message as to what type of position the individual is pursuing. Think of your elevator pitch as speed dating. First, determine your ice breaker, a unique fun fact that will grab the attention of your audience. Then, follow it up with a substantive fact or past success and finally, bring it home with a concluding statement that articulates how you plan to deliver business building value in a specific role in a specific industry, category or even organization. Elevator pitches are not just for use in elevators. You may need it at every toss and turn of your career transition journey, so develop it and perfect it well before you ever have to use it.

Collamer, N. (2013, February 4). The Perfect Elevator Pitch To Land A Job. Forbes. https://www.forbes.com/sites/nextavenue/2013/02/04/the-perfect-elevator-pitch-to-land-a-job/#1bb09ac51b1d

BRANDING BEGINS WITH YOUR EMAIL ADDRESS

"I suppose the best brand is being yourself."

–Leslie Higgins in Ted Lasso

How can something as simple as your choice of email address impact your job search as well as have a significant impact on your network? An email address is important in today's digital marketplace. Your email address is literally the "key" that will provide access to contact and collaboration. There are two important aspects that you must consider when establishing your email address. The first is portability and the second is branding. For portability, we must avoid the pitfall of creating an email address that is specific to your carrier or internet supplier. An example of such would be johndoe@ verizon.net. What happens if you move or decide to take advantage of a less costly carrier plan? Phone numbers are portable from carrier-to-carrier, but email addresses are not? The reason for this is if you ever change your carrier, you have now lost your digital identity and the ability for your network members to communicate with you. The second concern is branding and the image you are seeking to project. We suggest first name and last name @ email provider (example – Gmail). Over the years, we have received many emails that were either unprofessional and/or had started out well, but there must have been many John Doe's so they became johndoe9928@ verizon.net. Imagine the chance of someone mistyping this email address and if they do, chances are they will just think you already found a job or are no longer interested instead of following-up with you further once they don't hear back. Also, we have seen candidates sink their candidacy because their email was not consistent with a professional image. We actually received a resume with beachboy69@hotmail.com and many other email addresses that just aren't professional in nature. Finally, many individuals today are concerned with ageism. Please do not use an email like johndoe@aol.com which would project that you haven't kept up with technology. So, in the end, suffice to say email addresses do matter, so take the time to create one that will be consistent with your branding and be an asset to you.

MANAGE YOUR MEDIA PRESENCE

*"We get to live in a time that we get
to use social media as a tool."*

–Gigi Hadid

Effectively managing your media presence is a key factor of success for every job search. Most employers conduct a digital search of your owned media channels as part of their due diligence in the hiring process. When you start a job search, simply Google yourself. You want to learn if there is any information that comes back that can harm your candidacy. We have seen individuals who find out that someone else has their same name and unfortunately have done some bad things that would harm their candidacy if a potential employer confused the candidate for the individual who had committed the transgressions. If you find this, you can proactively alert a potential employer that this situation exists and ensure and possible share evidence that it is not you and hopefully prevent it from harming your candidacy. Today, many individuals are open and vocal about politics and other issues, but feel it is appropriate on a personal site such as Facebook. Our lives are now an open book, and many have strong opinions on politics, current events and even sports. So, do yourself a favor as there is such a small difference between the candidates that the hiring manager is considering for filling the opportunity and ensure there is nothing out there digitally to hurt your candidacy or give your opponents the edge in selection over you. We have seen candidates not selected because of personal information that they have posted on their social media channels and the potential employer felt that it wasn't consistent with their image or brand. The bottom line is to be very selective and think through what you post and check what may come back in a search of your name at the beginning of a job search so you have enough time to address, in some cases clean up, what a potential employer will see so it doesn't tank your candidacy inadvertently.

GET VISUAL WITH YOUR RESUME

"Create your own visual style... let it be unique for yourself and yet identifiable for others."

–Orson Welles

Infographic resumes are a new approach to communicating your capabilities. If you want to differentiate yourself and your candidacy, you should consider creating a visual resume. However, we would like to add a disclaimer - as visual resumes are new some may be impressed with the creative and innovative format, but some, may not. Therefore, please also share a version of your resume in a traditional format. This way you don't run the risk of your candidacy being stopped as you "didn't meet the requirements."

Some great sources to research if you want to explore designing and developing a visual resume are:

- Visualize.me
- Visual CV
- Visual Resume

- Hashtag CV
- Ineedresu.me
- Kick resume
- Zety
- ResumeUp
- Resume by Canva

Resumonk

INVEST QUALITY TIME ON YOUR RESUME SPECS

*"If you call failures experiments,
you can put them in your resume and
claim them as achievements."*

–Mason Cooley

You need to invest some quality time into creating a well thought through and comprehensive master resume. This master resume will contain the very important PARs (See PARs Lesson 93) which will be critical to not only your resume but branding and interviewing activities as well. Then, as each opportunity arises you want to develop a quality submission and retain the version of the resume that you submitted to the specific opportunity identified in your master tracking sheet. Again, it is about quality, not quantity. Anyone can submit into the black hole the techniques outlined here in this book. If followed appropriately, you will get quality results (interviews, follow-up interviews, job offers). And, as importantly, you will minimize the time you have to spend in transition dealing with the uncertainty. Do this correctly and get it done and behind you and land successfully in a job you will enjoy sooner rather than later.

CUT TO THE POINT
WITH YOUR COVER LETTER

*"Have a strong opening statement that makes clear why
you want the job and what you bring to the table."*

–Amy Gallo

We get asked by candidates to review their cover letters before they submit it as part of a formal job application. The organization or company requesting a cover letter is not asking for your biography which many candidates like to submit. Many candidates like to cram as much information about themselves into the second paragraph of a cover letter and what they don't squeeze in, they extend to a third paragraph. Your resume already provides much of this information so there is no need to be repetitive. Not only does the potential employer not want to receive and read all of this information, but by writing at length you increase your chances of making errors. Instead, commit to an efficient and effective three paragraph cover letter. In the first paragraph simply explain why you are sending the letter including the exact title of the position you are applying for.

In your second paragraph, you want to feature a few personal and professional highlights. Finally, you should conclude your letter with a third paragraph in which you thank the individual for their review and consideration. That is all you need to write in a cover letter and nothing more.

Gallo, A. (2014, February 4). *How To Write A Cover Letter*. Harvard Business Review . https://hbr.org/2014/02/how-to-write-a-cover-letter

PROACTIVELY REQUEST REFERENCES

*"The way to bring about change is to be
proactive and active."*

–Octavia Spencer

There are two types of references - the first is one you can do proactively and have on your LinkedIn Profile as a recommendation and the second is an individual you provide directly to a potential employer at their request that they can contact. You should proactively seek out and have several individuals provide recommendations on your LinkedIn profile. This will differentiate you from other LinkedIn profiles that don't have recommendations and if you work with those who are willing to provide you a recommendation you can work with them to address different aspects that will help proactively validate some of your competencies and capabilities. We have seen some instances where recruiters and potential employers simply accepted the recommendations instead of requesting and contacting references. Additionally, you need to collaborate with your references to effectively leverage your relationship:

- Gain their agreement to serve as a reference on your behalf

- Review any opportunity that you will supply them as a reference in advance recapping the opportunity, who it is with, and why you would make a great candidate

- Keep them informed through each stage of the process so they understand and can be prepared and anticipate the contact reaching out

- Remember to thank them for their support regardless of the outcome and offer to reciprocate on their behalf if ever needed

READY YOUR RESEARCH

"Research is creating new knowledge."

–Neil Armstrong

"Before going to a job interview, you should spend time finding out about the company. When you research a company, you're looking for information that tells you about its culture, history, and achievements. You should also be looking for information on what the company offers in terms of its services or products. How long has the company been in business? How have the company's products or services changed or improved over the years? Has the company expanded its business to other locations or parts of the world? Who is the CEO of the company? Knowing the answers to these kinds of questions can help you make a good impression on your interviewers." This excerpt from a blog post could not state any better the critical importance research must play in your job prospecting strategy. Whether you conducted extensive research or not as part of your past role and responsibilities, it should be one of your primary focuses now. From conducting initial research about past classmates and colleagues to researching job openings and opportunities, research should consume a significant amount of your time during your transition second only to networking. In fact, once you have uncovered an opportunity and are invited to compete for it, that's when the real research just gets started. From the moment you secure a formal or even informational interview, you need to start to dial-up your depth of research. The moment you get an interview on the calendar, you need to research everything about that individual - where did they go to college, where did they work prior to their current role, what type of content do they post on social media, what types of activities do they participate in outside of work, have they been quoted or featured in the media? Even search for videos of them presenting or conducting media interviews to better understand their verbal communication style and the types of messages they prioritize and deliver. You then need to conduct the same kind of due diligence on the company they work for - who are their clients, who is their competition, what have they been in the news for lately, what are the most pressing concerns in their industry or category? Then, and only then, will you have conducted enough research to have prepared yourself to achieve success. However, don't fool yourself by thinking a couple of Google searches is conducting in-depth research. You can never conduct enough research.

Have An Interview? 6 Reasons Why Research Is Key. Post University. (2021, January 4). https://post.edu/blog/have-an-interview-6-reasons-why-research-is-key/

PRIORITIZE PREPARING FOR YOUR INTERVIEW

"Before anything else, preparation is the key to success."

–Alexander Graham Bell

Effective preparation for your interview will be critical to your success:

- Thoroughly review the job specifications and clearly communicate the value that you will deliver

- Work through your PARs specific to the needs of this position

- Research the organization thoroughly and develop some insightful questions for those who will be interviewing you

- Have a draft of your "Thank You" letter so you can fit in specifics from the interview to again strengthen your candidacy. If you are interviewed by more than one person, personalize each thank you letter to each individual

- Have a list of "must ask" questions, allowing you to get the information you need in order to consider the job even more than you already do

- Ensure you know exactly where you are traveling to for the interview, and when possible, do a dry run the weekend prior to the location

- Leave extra time to travel to the interview as there is only "on-time" or late, and you never want to be late. You have only one chance to make a strong first impression and being late is not going to help you do that

- Don't discuss anything regarding the interview with anyone (recruiter, family member, etc.) until you are off-premise of the employer and out of earshot of anyone that can be associated with the employer

- Pick up a book on body language so that you can read non-verbal cues from the interviewer as you are interacting with them

- Practice interviewing techniques and questions in advance of the interview, but during the interview carefully interact, listen intently and follow cues from the interviewer

- If you have been able to make a contact at the employer through your network, ask your contact about the attire appropriate for interviewing- formal suit or business casual

- Remember that everything you bring with you to the interview helps the interviewer form an opinion of you. If you are an older candidate and are saying you are tech savvy and pull out a flip phone, it's not going to go over well

ASK HIGH-QUALITY QUESTIONS

"A prudent question is one half of wisdom."

–Francis Bacon

In a column titled, "10 Ridiculously Smart Questions You Should Ask In A Job Interview," Rachel Weingarten writes, "You've been so busy preparing to answer questions, that you're forgetting to show the curiosity that lets interviewers see what you really want to know. After all, even if every single one of your responses are flawless and on point, by not asking a question or two of your interviewer, you run the risk of coming across as generic." However, you can't just ask any question or two. You need to ask smart, thought-provoking, high-quality questions.

- As your organization competes for new business and clients, how do you articulate why prospects should choose your firm over the others?
- Who are your biggest competitors and how does the company plan to stay ahead?

- With the marketplace evolving so rapidly, what specific areas will the company focus on over the next several years to continue to innovate and transform?
- What's the biggest opportunity for growth over the next few years?
- In your own words, how would you describe your company's culture?
- How will you measure success of the new hire in this role a year from now?
- What keeps you up at night with respect to your role, responsibilities delivering business impact and value?
- What is the greatest impact the company has had on the industry?

These types of high-quality questions are smart and strategic in nature. They are also the type of questions that transform a job interview into a collaborative conversation. Often, the candidate who is selected for the job is the one who those conducting the interviews had the most compelling "conversation" with, not the most compelling interview. A senior marketing communications executive remarked, "I'm convinced a candidate's questions, not answers, separate them from the pack. By asking insightful questions, the candidate is inviting the interviewer to engage in a more authentic conversation that reveals what it would be like to work with this candidate."

Weingarten, R. (2017, August 1). *10 Questions You Should Always Ask In A Job Interview*. Ladders. https://www.theladders.com/career-advice/questions-job-interview

PHONE INTERVIEWS: ARTICULATE YOUR ATTITUDE

*"The thought process can never be complete
without articulation."*

–Stephen King

Phone interviews are good and bad. They are good in that they just basically gave you a gift of making the interview an open book test and bad in that you need to be prepared and have an understanding of the nuances of a phone interview versus virtual and in-person interviews so that you can take advantage of these differences and use them for your success. Many label the phone interview the "ironing board interview" and that's because what many do is set up their materials on an ironing board in front of a mirror. The ironing board is long and narrow and will allow you to lay out several reference materials in an order and way you can quickly lay your hands on them. By doing this in front of a mirror, the suggestion is that you smile the entire time as having the visual feedback helps you to remember and come across better. Also, standing while you do the interview has been proven to help you project your voice better and make a better impression. One point to remember as you cannot see the interviewer and they can't see you; it is critical that you employ great active listening skills and listen for tone in their responses and if you hear or need a question explained further remember to do so rather than potentially looking like you don't know the answer. Also, being that this interview method requires a very strong sense of sound, chances are the interviewer can hear what's going on in your background. It's best to be up front if there may be any unexpected sounds like a dog barking, or a family member being loud in another room. The bottom line is that with a phone interview, the potential employer cannot see you, your body language or how you are dressed. So, they are making their decision based on your articulation and confidence as well as the answers and content you deliver. Finally, always remember that technology plays a critical role in a phone interview. If you have a poor phone connection, it may eliminate you from the process because that poor cell phone connection will not allow you to articulate with confidence. Test out your connection in advance and proactively think through a backup alternative in case problems arise.

SCRIPT YOUR VIDEOCONFERENCE SESSION

*"You need to make mistakes in rehearsal because that's
how you find out what works and what doesn't."*

–Clarke Peters

Through this book, we stress the importance of conducting extensive research to prepare for every interview. However, a videoconference session via Zoom, Teams or Google Meet requires some additional considerations:

- Plan where you intend to physically take the videoconference call and ensure that the background (the wall behind you) aligns with the image that you want to project and also ensure the lighting is appropriate.

- Set-up a dry run with your laptop and ensure that it's positioned so the screen is looking directly at you not low or high.

- During your dry run, conduct an actual dress rehearsal, putting on the clothing that you intend to wear during the interview so that you can see how it displays.

- Make sure all pop-ups like instant messenger and mail notification are temporarily disabled on your device so that they don't interfere with your session.

- Conduct a test interview with someone using the videoconference service to ensure that you have tested and ironed out any technical issues or connection problems.

- Even after you prepare and script your videoconference session, you have to remember that the interviewer will be driving the interview so be prepared and ready to adapt as they conduct the interview.

If the meeting invite indicates that a product will be used like Zoom, Teams, Google Meet or something similar, make sure you check that the device you plan to use meets the required system requirements and download that application in advance and gain some familiarity with the product so you can navigate it seamlessly during the interview.

BE THE GREATEST INTERVIEWEE

*"If a man is called to be a streetsweeper,
he should sweep streets even as Michelangelo
painted or Beethoven composed music, or
Shakespeare wrote poetry. He should sweep
streets so that the hosts of heaven and earth
will pause to say, here lived a great
streetsweeper who did his job well."*

–Martin Luther King Jr.

If it's been a while since you interviewed for a position (interviewing candidates to consider hiring them doesn't count) or if you are new to interviewing, there are numerous things that will help you. Seek out resources to prepare you: engage a career coach, tap your university alumni office who supply interview training, or engage a job search or networking group that offers interview preparation advice and training – TAKE ADVANTAGE OF IT! Also, you can ask friends, family or contacts if they are hiring managers and most will be willing to run you through a mock interview and provide you feedback. You can also video the interview so you can then watch it and do your own self critique identifying strengths and weaknesses to work on. You must do your homework. Research the employer and have good questions prepared that you can ask. Review the job requisitions extensively and your T Letter so you understand the evidence you provided as to why you were a match so you can speak to the PARs that you shared. Make sure when you close your interview that you reinforce your interest in the position and ask what the next steps and timeline are for a final decision. This is critical for your follow-up. Immediately following the interview, compose a well-thought through personalized "Thank You" note to send to each interviewer. If a recruiter was involved, once you have left the interview and the potential employer's premises are in a place where you have privacy outside of the employer's offices or immediate surroundings, call the recruiter and debrief them on how the interview went.

USE BODY LANGUAGE TO YOUR ADVANTAGE

"Body language is a very powerful tool. We had body language before we had speech, and apparently, 80% of what you understand in a conversation is read through the body, not the words."

–Deborah Bull

Understanding body language is another critical skill needed during your job search and throughout life even in today's world of Zoom interviews. It is critical that you purchase a book on this topic and truly understand the fundamentals of body language prior to your interview. As you are speaking with the interviewer, use good eye contact. Also, upon meeting the interviewer provide a strong and confident handshake upon meeting them. As you are answering questions, it is important that you carefully study the interviewer's body language and maintain eye contact. If they seem to be growing disinterested with your response, you may not be on point, or your answer may be too long. Remember to be concise. Think of yourself conducting a three-minute live television interview where you need to answer each question in concise sound bites. If the interviewer seems frustrated or distracted, you may want to be proactive and let them know that you can wait or step outside their office if they have something urgent that they need to attend to immediately. This may make a significant difference. If they are distracted, they may not even remember interviewing you. Bring copies of your resume and T Letter and offer to provide them as the interviewer may not have them and it shows you are prepared. Be concise in your responses. If the interviewer wants to delve further, they will ask. If not, your initial response delivered the answer to the question they asked.

INFORMATIONAL INTERVIEWS MAKE FOR A GREAT DRESS REHEARSAL

"In other words, informational interviews are not just for college students, nor should they be left for that moment when you desperately need a job. That's because at the heart of the informational interview is the act of building long-term relationships and collaborating with others in an exchanging of ideas."

–Stephen Dupont

We hear Gen Z candidates regularly say, "it's only an informational interview." Informational interviews are incredibly valuable, and you should proactively schedule as many as you can, no matter your generation. Just about any executive will take the time to meet with a job seeker especially if the meeting is labeled an "informational interview." Treat informational interviews as dress rehearsals for formal interviews in the future. From the research you conduct and the questions you prepare to the way you dress and the manner in which you make the strongest possible first impression, informational interviews can serve as your off-Broadway performance before you make it to the big time. It not only serves as a chance to rehearse, but you are expanding your network in the process and don't be surprised if you receive a call back. If you make the right impression with that executive across the desk, they will most likely consider you for a future opening at their organization. Additionally, if you are looking to transition teams or make an internal move, traditionally, you as an employee may be required to let your current manager know that you have expressed interest in another opportunity. Soliciting informal coffee chats with internal leaders may be a great help with learning more about how that operates, allowing you to create a vision of yourself in the new environment, on a new team. The more you connect internally can also be a great dress rehearsal.

Dupont, S. (2017, June 16). *Leveraging The Power Of Informational Interviews*. Medium. https://medium.com/career-relaunch/leveraging-the-power-of-informational-interviews-91bd9c4fcdc0

DRESS THE PART

*"You have to dress for the job you want,
not the job you have..."*

–Austin Kleon

One of the most frequent questions asked before a candidate conducts a job interview whether in-person or virtual is, "What should I wear?" While it seems like a simple ask, it is actually very important. Before you visit any organization, ask and learn the appropriate work attire, as the rules of fashion in the workplace have changed significantly over the past several years, especially after the pandemic. If you are meeting with investment firms on Wall Street, a suit and tie may be the best choice of attire while if you are interviewing with a social media or advertising agency, blue jeans and sneakers may be appropriate. You do not want to make the mistake of being overdressed or underdressed. We know one creative marketing agency who will be turned off if a candidate arrives in a suit and tie. You don't want your fashion choice to become the focus of the interview whether you are sitting in the potential employer's office or in your living room. The bottom line is to be proactive and ask your point-of-contact at the company (in many cases that is the internal recruiter) for the most appropriate way to dress. It will contribute to making a strong first impression.

INTERVIEW EMPLOYERS

"Be so good they can't ignore you."

–Steve Martin

When you finally get the email or call for a job interview, shift your mindset and think about how you are going to interview your potential employer. Too often, candidates focus solely on the types of questions they are going to be asked and how they are going to answer them. The secret to a successful interview is to turn it into a conversation. The way to do that is to develop smart questions. You want to avoid feeling like you just sweated through an interrogation and instead, enjoy a collaborative conversation. Everyone takes pride in speaking about themselves, their organization and their project and campaign experience. The key is you need to ask the interviewer those types of personal and professional questions in a way that naturally elevates the interview into a conversation. One effective way to do that is to conduct as much advance research as possible about the individuals who are interviewing you and the organization they work for. Another is having a list of questions to ask once you get closer to the end of the interview. If done right, the recruiter will have informed you of the duration of the interview (make sure to confirm prior to), so paying close attention to the length of your answers, while making sure there is enough time to secure all the information you need, will be a tremendous help, and show that you're interested in the role. When it comes to discussing your candidacy amongst the others on the interview panel, they will for sure remember those who were engaged and asked questions.

CULTURE IS
CRITICALLY IMPORTANT

*"Corporate culture matters. How management
chooses to treat its people impacts everything
for better or for worse."*

–Simon Sinek.

No two company cultures are the same especially in today's remote work environment as the culture of an organization is determined by a variety of unique elements including the individuals who currently work there, the management team that leads the organization as well as the history of the organization, rituals and even the unspoken language that is only understood within a company. You not only need to uncover the culture of an organization during your interview process, but you need to determine the best culture for you. Do you excel in an environment where they take a laissez faire approach or country club approach, or would you prefer a more structured organization where hard work and long hours and even weekend duty is rewarded? Will you perform better in an atmosphere that is highly social and colleagues prioritize outings and events inside and outside the building or do you lean toward an environment where the exclusive focus is the task at hand and socializing is not important to you? Are you at your best working in a physical office or do you thrive working remotely two or more days a week? Once you determine the type of culture where you believe you will thrive, you then need an organization that can deliver that cultural experience to you.

CULTURAL COMPETENCY AND INCLUSION

"A diverse mix of voices leads to better discussions, decisions, and outcomes for everyone."

–Sundar Pichai

Cultural competency, a lifelong journey of understanding and appreciating the beliefs, values, and practices of diverse cultures, stands as a cornerstone of fostering a more inclusive society. This ongoing process is crucial for bridging gaps and promoting understanding among individuals from various cultural backgrounds. The world is more inclusive than it's ever been, and it serves to enhance communication and empathy among people from different cultures, breaking down stereotypes and discrimination. Within the evolving industry, it is Gen Z professionals, along with others, who place a huge emphasis on the type of culture they want to be immersed in and want to be sure that the organization they choose to work with fosters that. It cultivates an environment that is both inviting and supportive, fostering innovation, informed decision-making, and ultimately, heightened productivity and profitability. Inclusion, on the other hand, embodies the act of crafting spaces where everyone, regardless of their background, feels genuinely welcomed, respected, and valued. It revolves around creating an atmosphere conducive to personal growth and success. The two are needed in order to create a positive environment for you and your team.

Cultural competency and inclusion share an intrinsic link, both serving as integral elements in the pursuit of a fair and equitable society. Mercedes Martin and Billy Vaughn stated, "Regardless of whether our attitude toward cultural differences match our behavior, we can benefit from improving our cross-cultural effectiveness." When we embrace cultural competency, we gain a deeper understanding of others' experiences, nurturing a mindset that naturally gravitates towards inclusivity. To become more culturally competent and inclusive, you can take several steps:

- Learn about different cultures: Invest time in understanding the customs and traditions of various cultures.

- Embrace new experiences: Be open to learning from diverse encounters and perspectives by joining Employee Resource Groups (ERG) and going to companywide programs where you can not only be a part of the conversation and change, but you can add to it.

- Challenge biases and assumptions: Self-reflection and addressing preconceived notions are pivotal. Everyone has their bias, whether its unconscious or conscious. Feel empowered to express your thoughts, but always remain respectful.

- Respect diverse beliefs and values: Honor the uniqueness of others' perspectives. Put yourself in their shoes, as you would want them to do the same for you.

- Advocate for the marginalized: Stand up for those facing exclusion or discrimination.

Ultimately, cultural competency and inclusion are not just individual or organizational endeavors; they are the cornerstones of creating a fairer and more equitable world. We all have a responsibility to be aware and make a positive difference. It all starts with you.

Martin, M., & Vaughn, B. (n.d.). *Cultural Competence: The Nuts & Bolts of Diversity & Inclusion.* Diversity Officer Magazine. https://diversityoff icermagazine.com/cultural-competence/cultural-competence-the-nuts-bolts-of-diversity-inclusion-2/

THANK YOU NOTES
GET NOTICED

"In fact, fair or not, most hiring managers pay very close attention to whether you write a thank you email after the interview."

–Alyse Kalish

You have worked hard to meet people and when you have met them, you have made the commitment to nurture the relationship. Now, do one simple thing that will make you stand out from the competition – send a thank you email – better yet, handwrite and mail a thank you note. Yes, handwrite a thank you note. In a world of texting and templated email correspondence, take the time to invest in branded thank you cards and write a personal note to the individuals who took time out of their schedules to meet with you and share their insights, lessons, and recommendations – and send it in a timely manner. When you write your note, personalize it based on the topics you discussed in the meeting so that the recipient knows you actively listened. If they discussed a vacation they are taking or their favorite sports team, refer to it in your note. Believe it or not, your thank you note will last well beyond an email "thank you." The recipient will not only be pleasantly surprised, but they will socialize and share with colleagues. It is a very simple approach to break through the clutter and stand out among a crowded field of candidates. In a November 30, 2022 article in *Harvard Business Review*, Christopher Littlefield captures it well when he writes, "Hiring managers understand that candidates may be interviewing for multiple jobs at the same time. Busy themselves, leaders don't want to invest time in a candidate who is not invested in the role they're hiring for. A thank you message confirms that you're both interested and excited about the role and worth following up with."

Kalish, A. (2023, July 25). *How to Write a Thank You Email After an Interview (With Samples!)*. The Muse. https://www.themuse.com/advice/how-to-write-an-interview-thankyou-note-an-email-template

Littlefield, C. (2022, November 30). *How To Write A Thank You Email After An Interview*. Harvard Business Review. https://hbr.org/2022/11/how-to-write-a-thank-you-email-after-an-interview

PART VI

Thrive In A Multigenerational Workplace

ALL GENERATIONS DELIVER VALUE IN THE WORKPLACE

*"Older and wiser voices can help you find the right path,
if you are only willing to listen."*

–Jimmy Buffett

There are an unprecedented five generations collaborating alongside each other in some workplaces today. Ranging from members of The Silent Generation, the youngest who are in their mid-70s, to the newest members of the workforce, Generation Z, the oldest who are in their mid-20s. In between are baby boomers, Gen X and millennials. In a June 12, 2023 article in *Forbes*, Dinette Koolhaas writes, "For the first time in history, five different generations are working together. At one end, members of the Silent Generation (1925-1945) are capping off the final years of careers that spanned monumental technological changes. At the other, Generation Z (2001-2020) employees are entering the workforce having never known a world without the internet. These two age groups, along with baby boomers, Gen Xers, and millennials, are working side-by-side. Though these generationally diverse workforces are sometimes portrayed as predominantly discordant, or full of challenges, it is to the distinct benefit of companies and leaders to leverage the unique talents, insights and outlooks of multi-generational employees." The reason that Koolhaas highlights that it is a benefit to leverage the unique talents of each generation is because each and every generation delivers value to the workplace. In a Live Career Study, 89 percent of employees consider generational diversity a positive element of work today and 87 percent consider the opportunity to learn from each other as a benefit of a multigenerational workplace. In the next few lessons, we will showcase those values. It is critically important to comprehend that no matter the generation you represent, you deliver value that complements the value your colleagues from other generations bring to the workplace. Recognizing generational value is the first step in thriving in today's multigenerational workplace. Members of The Silent Generation were born as many as 50 years before their Gen Z colleagues, but they can each learn from each other in a way that delivers measurable business-building value to their employer. In a February 17, 2021 article for *USA Today* that John Boitnott authored, he writes, "When looking at who to hire, don't put as much importance on age and stereotypes about skill levels. Go beyond by meeting each applicant where they're at, with a focus on the undervalued skills both older and younger workers may bring to the table. It will give new insight into what the future of your company could look like."

Koolhaas, D. (2023, June 12). *How To Wield The Power Of A Multi-Generational Workforce*. Forbes. https://www.forbes.com/sites/forbes humanresourcescouncil/2023/06/12/how-to-wield-the-power-of-a-multi-generational-workforce/?sh=49c967a93143

Boitnott, J. (2021, February 17). *From Work Experience To Organizational Knowledge: Here Are 5 Advantages Older Workers Have Over Other Job Candidates.* USA Today. https://www.usatoday.com/story/money/usaandmain/2021/02/17/advantages-older-workers-job-candidates/4482652001/

EXPERIENCE COUNTS

*"I want to be thoroughly used up when I die,
for the harder I work, the more I live. I rejoice in life
for its own sake. Life is no brief candle to me. It is
a sort of splendid torch which I have got a hold of
for the moment, and I want to make it burn brightly
as possible before handing it to future generations."*

–George Bernard Shaw

Members of The Silent Generation (born between 1928-1945), baby boomers (born between 1946-1964) and Generation X (born between 1965-1980), spent many decades in a traditional workplace setting prior to 2020 where they commuted to a physical office building five or more days a week, worked in an office from nine-to-five and beyond and adopted new technologies as they were introduced to tech ranging from conference calls and the fax machine to email and videoconferencing. As Dinette Koolhaas highlights in a June 12, 2023 column in *Forbes*, "Older generations bring deep knowledge, industry experience and the perspective gained by years in the workforce." That is a value that Gen Z can't bring to the table as they haven't been in the workforce long enough. As members of the oldest generations – The Silent Generation, baby boomers and Gen X – approach the back end of their careers, they have substantive experience including many failures, successful case studies and lessons learned, all of which can inform and inspire new programs, campaigns, and initiatives. Additionally, now in the third, fourth or fifth decades of their career, they have amassed a well-established professional network. In other words, they have many connections across many industries and organizations which can be leveraged for the benefit of their current employer. Finally, the oldest members of the workforce possess historical knowledge that just can't be matched. They have historical context for past customers, clients and programs that in many cases is not available via A.I. or a Google search. The bottom line is that experience counts, and members of The Silent Generation, baby boomers and Gen X deliver valuable experience each and every day in the workplace.

Koolhaas, D. (2023, June 12). *How To Wield The Power Of A Multi-Generational Workforce*. Forbes. https://www.forbes.com/sites/forbes humanresourcescouncil/2023/06/12/how-to-wield-the-power-of-a-multi-generational-workforce/?sh=49c967a93143

MILLENNIALS ARE THE BRIDGE TO SUCCESS

"Millennials are the largest generation in today's workforce. Millennials have changed the traditional style of leadership by having different values and expectations from their leaders. Communication, relationship-building and empowerment are some of the key components in millennials preferred leadership styles."

–Jennifer Post

Prior to the pandemic, the Society for Human Resource Management wrote the following about millennials on July 9, 2019, "Millennials, the generation born between 1981 and 1996, have grown up in a rapidly evolving world. Millennials are ambitious, quick to learn and are resilient team players. They are a generation that want to feel valued and are determined to make an impact on the business world." Fast forward to 2024 and millennials have evolved and advanced significantly up the corporate ladder. They are no longer entry level employees. They currently represent the largest generation in the workforce. Gen Z has replaced them as the newest members of the workplace. With increased responsibility, we believe that millennials are the all-important bridge that connects older generations with younger generations at the workplace. The millennial bridge is critically important for employers today. If that bridge buckles and breaks, a company could go out of business. Millennials effectively manage up and down. They report to older generations who are sitting in the c-suite and other leadership positions, and they have been empowered to mentor and manage the newest employees, Gen Z. That's a tremendous responsibility which results in delivering significant value to their employer. Simultaneously, millennials aspire to evolve and advance in their respective careers. They have set their sights on becoming the next generation of corporate leaders as older generations ride off into the sunset. They will do that by effectively managing Gen Zers who will replace millennials as they are promoted to leadership roles. Across generations in the workplace, there may be no generation more valuable today than millennials. They are the bridge that connects generations and which a company's transformation, innovation, and success crosses over.

Post, J. (2023, February 21). *What Does Modern Leadership Really Mean?*. Business. https://www.business.com/articles/leadership-styles-millennials/

Khanna, A. (2019, July 9). *Why Companies Should Engage with Millennials*. Society For Human Resource Management. https://www.shrm.org/resourcesandtools/hr-topics/employee-relations/pages/why-should-companies-engage-with-millennials.aspx

EMPOWER GEN Z EMPLOYEES AS ZEOS

"There's never a right answer with this generation: It's made up of so many different people and audiences, but at the same time, we're all human. Start having conversations with Gen Z and that will start bridging these gaps."

**–Andrew Roth,
Founder, dcdx**

Mark Beal, one of this book's co-authors, authored a book in 2023 titled, *ZEO: Introducing Gen Z, The New Generation of Leaders*. While Gen Zers, or as Mark identifies them as ZEOs, do not have the extensive experience, vast professional networks, successful case studies and lessons learned that older generations deliver to the workplace, members of Gen Z are digital natives and early tech adopters who are an unprecedented generation of entrepreneurs. Throughout the pandemic, Gen Zers demonstrated tremendous resilience and the ability to seamlessly and adapt as they were forced to transition to remote learning with no planning or preparation. In a July 10, 2023 article in *Fast Company* titled, "Managing Gen Z: Fast Company's 142-Point Guide For Leaders," Mark described Gen Z's value to the workplace in this way. "Gen Z's entrepreneurial mindset is unprecedented. They have launched startups, side hustles, companies, and nonprofit charitable organizations as early as middle school by leveraging the digital and social media platforms and technology which has been readily available to them at a young age and which they eagerly adopt. They want to take that same entrepreneurial approach on the first day that they join a company as an employee. Leaders and employers who recognize this truth about Gen Z will flourish and succeed." While Gen Z will be the youngest generation in the workplace until Gen Alpha arrives in a decade, they will deliver measurable business-building value that will usher in innovation and transformation as long as older generations empower them as ZEOs.

Gupta, S. (2023, February 25). *What Really Makes Gen Z Different From Older Generations? We Asked A 24-Year-Old Brand Consultant*. Fast Company. https://www.fastcompany.com/90855007/gen-z-different-than-older-generations-brand-consultant

Lidsky, D. (2023, July 10). *Managing Gen Z: Fast Company's 142-Point Guide For Leaders*. Fast Company. https://www.fastcompany.com/90918427/managing-gen-z-fast-companys-142-point-guide-for-leaders

MANAGE IMPOSTER SYNDROME

"Remember that if you are feeling like an impostor, it means you have some degree of success in your life that you are attributing to luck. Try instead to turn that feeling into one of gratitude. Look at what you have accomplished in your life and be grateful for your achievements."

–Arlin Cuncic

Let's get deep for a few minutes. Find a place that makes you relaxed. Take a seat and think. Have you ever heard of Imposter Syndrome? Sure, you have! Most professionals know this term, but not all can overcome this challenge and get out of their own way. Imposter Syndrome is a common feeling of self-doubt that many people experience, especially when they are starting a new job or taking on a new challenge. Some of the most common traits include experiencing self-doubt, believing way more into luck than internal factors, undermining your own achievements or progress, setting ambitious goals, and experiencing disappointment when you don't reach them. Arlin Cuncic, MA, noted in an article, "It is estimated that

70% of people will experience at least one episode of this phenomenon at some point in their lives." Yes, that means it can, or it's already happened, or happening to you. This is where your self-reflection comes into play. Take a few seconds to think about the last time you doubted yourself. Better yet, ask yourself these questions:

- Do you respond well to constructive criticism, even when it's offered?
- Do you tend to minimize your own expertise, even when you surpass others in certain areas?
- Do you find yourself dwelling on even the slightest errors or imperfections in your work?

If your answer is "yes", then you are in the right place. Now that you have identified an area of improvement, you can begin to work on becoming a better version of yourself. Find someone to share your feelings with. Stop comparing yourself to others, especially when you utilize social media. Most importantly, have the confidence to never stop striving for greatness because only you can stop you from achieving the life and career you have always wanted!

Cuncic, A. (2023, May 22). *Imposter Syndrome: Why You May Feel Like a Fraud.* Very Well Mind. https://www.verywellmind.com/imposter-syndrome-and-social-anxiety-disorder-4156469

NEVER STOP NETWORKING

*"What good is livin' a life you've been given
if all you do is stand in one place?"*

–Kenny Chesney

We would be all be multi-millionaires one day if we trademarked a line for bumper stickers and t-shirts that read, "Help, I'm Networking and I Can't Stop!" So many individuals who are out of work, learn the importance of networking while they are in a career transition and in the job search mode, but then fall back to their former ways and don't network once they start their new job. They often claim that they have too much on their plate and use it as an excuse. However, there has never been such a rate and volume of change in business due to digital transformation as there is today. This is causing major disruptions in all industries. The way in which business is done is literally changing. With these disruptions, we are the ones who are usually bearing the brunt with employers going out of business, merging, consolidating and divesting. It is more important now than ever in our history that you dedicate time to growing and strengthening your network. Additionally, many families are facing higher costs due to increases in taxes, prices, education and insurance. Thus, individuals and families don't have the financial buffer they once had. Therefore, please follow these two best practices:

- After securing a new job, put your networking competency to work at your new employer with new colleagues, consultants and preferred vendors
- Outside of your new job, stay involved in attending professional associations, give back to the networking groups that helped you, attend expo events and grow contacts and nurture relationships

WORK HARD TO MEET PEOPLE

"Be curious. Not judgmental... Because if they were curious, they would've asked questions."

–Ted Lasso

David Siroty, a 30-year public relations veteran who has represented clients in categories ranging from sports to real estate, served as a guest lecturer and delivered a 60-minute presentation centered on one powerful theme, "Work Hard To Meet People." Siroty's challenge to his audience was to make it their full-time job now that they are at their new job to establish and grow their professional networks by taking every opportunity to meet and engage individuals of influence across their new company. The key is to be proactive in your approach and professional in your follow-up. Pick your head up from your phone and your many meetings, extend your hand, introduce yourself and engage in conversation. It will set you apart and leave a positive and lasting impression with your colleagues including those who you work with daily as well as those who may be in other parts of the company where you may aspire to work one day.

GET TO KNOW
YOUR WORK FAMILY

"Coming together is a beginning; keeping together is progress; working together is success."

–Henry Ford

Throughout your career, you will spend more time with your work family than your actual family. Jonathan Neman, Cofounder of Sweetgreen commented in Fast Company, "People don't work for companies, they work for people. We don't have company meetings – we have family meetings. (Fast Company, Feb 2017)" That sentiment has not changed with the switch to remote and hybrid work. With that, take an interest in your colleague's passions outside the office, their interests and even their own families. Of course, there is a balancing act when it comes to work and socializing, but we shouldn't act like robots. If you are working alongside colleagues, you should be able to have discussions about life outside work. Imagine all you can learn from colleagues across generations. Your colleagues will take notice when you show genuine interest in their lives outside the workplace. It can be as simple as knowing the name of their significant other and asking how he or she is doing or asking how their children are doing in sports or other activities. Taking some extra time to better understand what is in the hearts and minds of your colleagues and showing interest and concern is one way to forge stronger relationships with those you work with. After all, you are most likely spending 45 or more hours a week collaborating and problem solving so you might as well get to know each other. It will only lead to a more productive relationship with your work family.

RECRUIT YOUR RABBIS

*"A good mentor hopes you will move on.
A great mentor knows you will."*

–Leslie Higgins in Ted Lasso

Leading public relations executive Sammy Steinlight speaks regularly to college students who are preparing for their transition to their careers, and he consistently offers a piece of valuable career advice – "Recruit your rabbis." No, he is not suggesting they convert to Judaism. He is encouraging them to identify and secure several mentors who can guide them for the next decade or more as they launch and establish their careers. Identifying and securing mentors is a long-term strategic and smart approach to investing in your career and investing in relationships that will produce dividends for many years to come. As you advance in your career, identify individuals from all generations – ranging from a Gen X CEO to the Gen Z owner of a startup company – who can serve in this role of mentor and counselor. This is someone you already know, trust and have a collaborative relationship with.

It is important to not only formally recruit your mentor but officially invite them to serve in this role knowing this will be an on-going mutually beneficial relationship that could last for decades to come.

DRAFT YOUR TOP 5

*"Surround yourself with people who support you.
Find champions."*

–Sarah Gavron

We all know who we want to reach out to when things get tough, and you need a helping hand. As you continue your career path, there should be five people you can rely on to help you out. At that point, you should not let your pride get in the way of your success by asking for help. Say you lost your job right now. Who would you call? That is where your "Top 5" comes into play, quite literally.

Your "Top 5" are people who know you well, believe in you, and are willing to help you find a job. They could be former colleagues, mentors, friends, or family members. Tai Goodwin and Jenna Arcand wrote, "Evaluate your current network and get started filling in the gaps." You should always be in a place of self-evaluation and reflection, especially when it comes to your goals and the people in your circle of influence.

Having a "Top 5" is important because it can give you a big boost in your job search. When you need a job, you can reach out to your "Top 5" and ask them for help. They can:

- Put you in touch with people who are hiring.
- Give you feedback on your resume and cover letter.
- Help you practice your interviewing skills.
- Provide moral support during your job search.

Having a "Top 5" can also help you to stay positive and motivated during your job search. When you're feeling discouraged, you can reach out to your "Top 5" and they can help you to stay focused on your goals.

Here are some tips for drafting your "Top 5":

- Think about the people who know you well and believe in you.
- Choose people who are willing to help you find a job.
- Make sure your "Top 5" is diverse. This means having people from different industries, with different levels of experience, and from different backgrounds.
- Keep your "Top 5" updated. As you meet new people and build relationships, add them to your "Top 5."

If you don't have a "Top 5" yet start by reaching out to your former colleagues, mentors, friends, and family members. Let them know that you're looking for a job and ask them if they would be willing to help you.

Building a "Top 5" takes time and effort, but it is worth it. When you need a job, your "Top 5" can be a valuable resource. Attend industry events and networking meetups and get involved in professional organizations Keep your LinkedIn profile up-to-date and active and always be open to new opportunities. The more people you know and the more involved you are in your industry, the more likely you are to build a strong "Top 5."

Goodwin, T., & Arcand, J. (2022, November 9). *Top 10 People You Must Have In Your Network To Find A Job*. Work It Daily. https://www.workit daily.com/must-have-people-in-network/who-should-be-part-of-your-network

UNSPECTACULAR PREPARATION WILL BE THE KEY TO YOUR SUCCESS

"One important key to success is self-confidence. An important key to self-confidence is preparation."

–Arthur Ashe

Now that you have secured your next career opportunity, the work is really just beginning. Just as you prepared extensively for every informal meeting and formal interview by conducting significant research, continue to take that approach in advance of your official start date and every day of your new assignment. Now, your research should focus on your company, the competition, the industry and the responsibilities of your new position and the position above you. Like an athlete preparing for the upcoming season with early morning training when no one is watching, your unspectacular preparation as you onboard at your new company will serve as the foundation for your future success.

Ask your new manager to share any information in advance as you would welcome the opportunity to begin reviewing it and preparing for your new opportunity.

There are two great books to consider making the most of your new opportunity:

- *The First 90 Days: Proven Strategies for Getting Up to Speed Faster and Smarter, Updated and Expanded* by Michael D. Watkins
- *The New Leader's 100-Day Action Plan: How to Take Charge, Build or Merge Your Team* by George Bradt, Jayme A. Check and Jorge Pedraza

MAKE THE MOST OF
YOUR FIRST 100 DAYS
ON THE JOB AND BEYOND

"The primary task for the executive targeting first 100 days success is to set out the right strategic priorities and stay focused on them."

–Niamh O'Keeffe

"**W**ow! I hated networking and now that I landed my new job, I can't wait to just relax." Buzz – wrong!

Now, more than ever, it's important to continue networking with those people in the new organization that you just joined. Network with all those you meet at your new firm. Connect with coworkers, those you meet from other organizations, stakeholders, managers, executives, consultants, and even vendors. Publish content that demonstrates your thought leadership but make sure it is consistent with your firm's goals, objectives and positions. Continue your networking activities outside of work that helped you land the position. Set a career plan of where you want to be in five to 10 years with measurable goals you want to achieve. Commit to continuous learning. "It was critical not to just get the job, but immediately blow the doors off for my new employer so they know that they undoubtedly made the best decision," said PJ Brovak, a marketing communications professional. "As a result, I have already been positively asked to take on more responsibilities and have set myself up for success with the organization." Technology is disrupting every facet of business including how it is getting done. We all must become lifelong learners. Relying on a college degree and learnings that are years in the past will no longer be enough. Keep a close eye on innovation and determine how your position will be transformed by it. Automation will be the source of greatest change in the future and we will all experience it, so embrace it and learn how to exploit it for the benefit of your career.

APPLY THE 80/20 RULE

"Productivity is never an accident. It is always the result of a commitment to excellence, intelligent planning, and focused effort."

–Paul J. Meyer

Based on the title of this chapter, you may or may not have heard this term before. I challenge you to proceed with an open mind, and I promise that you will not have flashbacks of the moments when you questioned the legitimacy of math playing a significant role in the success of your career. The 80/20 rule, commonly known as the Pareto principle, asserts that 80% of results stem from 20% of causes. However, let's flip the script, as adaptation is key to winning the job game. Applied differently, the 80/20 rule suggests that 80% of your outcomes result from just 20% of your efforts. This implies the existence of crucial tasks vital to your success, which, when prioritized, yield the most significant results. In this context, consider the 80% as your top priority—critical tasks requiring your unique skills and knowledge that have the most substantial impact on your bottom line. Productivity and efficiency will determine everything from a promotion, raise, and longevity in your company. When you break the 2 sides (.80+.20), it will help identify how you can meet that statement we are all too family with; giving 100% of yourself every day. Sarah Laoyan describes the success of this strategy by saying, "To do this, list out all of the things that you need to get done that day. Then identify which of those tasks have the highest impact." Consistency in this daily practice will yield long-term benefits, resulting in a fruitful career.

The remaining 20% of your efforts can be dedicated to fostering creativity and self-improvement, enhancing your skills, and boosting efficiency to attain greater success. This segment may involve professional development, expanding your network by meeting colleagues within your organization or through professional networking platforms, or even engaging in practices such as meditation. By striking this balance between focused priority tasks and personal growth, you pave the way for a more prosperous and fulfilling career.

Laoyan, S. (2022, December 8). *Understanding The Pareto Principle (The 80/20 Rule)*. Asana. https://asana.com/resources/pareto-principle-80-20-rule

ALWAYS BE ACCOUNTABLE

"Leaders inspire accountability through their ability to accept responsibility before they place blame."

–Courtney Lynch

From developing your resume and applying for jobs to conducting interviews and eventually handling your first project at your next job, be accountable for every action along the way. While you will seek and receive support and assistance from your multigenerational network, ultimately, you will need to be accountable for every action you take... or don't take. For example, if you are assigned a project at work and you do not properly prepare by conducting in-depth research and asking questions about the project objectives, timeline, budget, deliverables and so much more, you can't blame anyone but yourself. Leverage the experiences and strengths of every generation on your team and at your company. Learn from failures and apply your learnings to the next interview opportunity. As you advance in your career, your level of accountability will evolve with greater responsibilities and more individuals to manage so have the mindset right from the onset that you are accountable for everything you do, and it will set you on the right path for the remainder of your career.

FINANCIAL PLANNING
AND BUDGETING

"It's clearly a budget. It's got a lot of numbers in it."

–George W. Bush

When you win the job, big or small, entry-level up to c-suite, financial planning and budgeting are essential tools for managing money effectively, for you or for someone else. Tracking your income and expenses helps you identify where you can save money, and do things like make purchases, investments, and yes, even pay off those student loans. The challenge is living in a consumerist environment where social media creates a fear of missing out (FOMO) and platforms such as Afterpay, Klarna, and Affirm, create opportunities for you to buy now and pay later. "The amount of money you bring in each month is an essential part of your budget and creates the foundation for how much you can afford to spend. Alexandria White said it best by stating, "Creating effective spending and saving habits will help create the future you want, and it is important to build this habit in your college years and early in your career." By doing so, you are setting yourself up for success and becoming financially stable.

Comparing budgeting to a sport is like playing a game where there are various strategies and moves to help you achieve your goal, which in this case is scoring points for your bank account and investments. Just like in sports, there's no one-size-fits-all approach to managing your money effectively. Different budgeting methods, such as zero-based budgeting, envelope budgeting, and app-based budgeting, offer various plays and calls to make. You have to figure out what works best for you, but don't be afraid to try different methods and stick to a goal. The process of creating a budget involves a few key steps. First, you set a financial goal that you want to achieve, much like setting your game plan. Microsoft Excel is a great start, especially as technology continues to evolve, this application will be a very important skill to master. Next, you track your income and expenses, similar to monitoring your team's performance. Then, you categorize your expenses, creating a playbook for how you allocate your funds. Finally, you put your budget into action. However, the most critical part of budgeting is sticking to your plan, just as it's crucial to execute your strategy in a game. Regularly track your spending and remain flexible because life can throw unexpected challenges. Don't forget to reward yourself when you achieve your financial goals because it will be done in your own way as a result of finding the right plays to make in order to achieve success.

White, A. (2023, January 10). *5 budgeting tips for college students that can help set you up for financial success*. CNBC. https://www.cnbc.com/select/budgeting-tips-for-college-students/

SURROUND YOURSELF WITH PEOPLE WHO CHALLENGE YOU

"Surround yourself with good people; surround yourself with positivity and people who are going to challenge you to make you better."

–Ali Krieger

This lesson, which you should follow throughout your entire career, came from Todd Rovak, the CEO of a consulting firm who was quoted in *The New York Times* when asked to give advice to college graduates, "Surround yourself with people who challenge you. It doesn't matter what the job is. Just put yourself in that environment as fast as possible." (February 1, 2017, New York Times). From your first entry-level position until you lead a company one day, you always want to be challenged by individuals that are smarter and more strategic and creative than you are at solving business challenges. These can be members of the c-suite who are baby boomers and Gen Xers as well emerging leaders who ae millennials and entry level employees who are members of

Generation Z. If you find you are no longer being challenged in your career, move on to a new position with another organization. It is these types of challenges from others that will not only test you, but also empower you to evolve throughout your career.

RESIST THE STATUS QUO & BE TRANSFORMATIVE

"The riskiest thing we can do is just maintain the status quo."

–Bob Iger

Research and learn about transformational leaders. These are individuals who are never satisfied with success and are always thinking about how to not only transform themselves but the organizations they lead. Microsoft's former Chief Marketing Officer, Grad Conn, said it best in *Fast Company*, "Learning is probably the most important currency you can have as a human. Companies will continue to hire and to value employees who can transform." (Fast Company, February 2017). As you set the tone or theme for your career, be transformative. Leaders who are transformative not only collaborate with colleagues and create change for the better, but they set a vision for their organization and work with their team to live and fulfill that vision. Even a young Gen Z executive can be transformative in their approach. They will most likely inherit tasks and assignments that have been handled by previous entry level executives. Instead of accepting the assignment and doing it the same way it has always been done, determine how the slightest change can improve the process. In other words, transform the status quo and improve the effectiveness of something that has become routine. If you take a transformative approach with the smallest assignment, as you evolve throughout your career, your transformative mindset will influence even greater change and impact as your responsibilities grow.

CONSISTENCY IS KEY TO SUCCESS

"Success isn't always about greatness.
It's about consistency. Consistent hard work
leads to success. Greatness will come."

–Dwayne 'The Rock' Johnson

We have seen many young interns and executives who have demonstrated flashes of excellence. However, flashes of excellence are not going to lead you to a successful career. If you believe as we do that success is a marathon, then you need to take a long-term view and achieve consistent performance and production at a high-level day in and day out. This begins with your first internship and job and runs right through your entire career. It means showing up daily whether in-person or remote with the goal of winning the day. Do not approach your career like a home run hitter who hits 40 home runs a year and strikes out every other time they are up to bat. Instead, aspire to be a 400 hitter who makes contact nearly every time they are up to the plate and hit for singles, doubles and triples. If you can be as consistent as a 400 hitter, you will be in control of your future and the career decisions you make.

WORK EFFECTIVELY IN A REMOTE OR HYBRID ROLE

"Focus on being productive instead of busy."

–Tim Ferriss

The transition to working from home has been a significant and swift change that many professionals have grappled with. This shift is part of the broader transformation in the dynamic job market, where remote work has become increasingly prevalent. The impact of this change extends beyond the professional realm, as even school systems adapted to virtual learning during the global pandemic. This forced many parents to juggle the responsibilities of their own jobs while facilitating their children's remote education. It was, and for some still is, a formidable adjustment and challenge. Indeed, it often felt like this transformation occurred almost overnight, reshaping the way we work and learn. Here are some tips on how to work remotely:

Set up a dedicated workspace. This could be a spare bedroom, a home office, or even a corner of your living room. Having a dedicated workspace will help you stay focused and productive.

- Set clear boundaries between work and personal time. It can be easy to blur the lines between work and personal time when you're working from home. Make sure to set aside specific times for work and for personal activities.

- Take breaks throughout the day. It's important to take breaks throughout the day, even if you're working from home. Get up and move around, or step outside for some fresh air.

- Stay connected with your team. It's important to stay connected with your team, even if you're not working in the same office. Use video conferencing, instant messaging, or other tools to stay in touch.

- Take care of yourself. It's important to take care of your physical and mental health when you're working from home. Make sure to get enough sleep, eat healthy foods, and exercise regularly.

This might sound simple, but it can be a challenge without the proper amount of self-discipline. Legendary athletes such as Mike Tyson and Deion Sanders preach the philosophy of having strong discipline and adapting to change in order to become the best. Not being given a playbook to navigate at work or in a remote space, you should consider these supplementary tips for a successful remote working experience:

Prioritize Organization: Effective organization is pivotal when working remotely. Implement tools like project management software, establish a systematic approach to document storage, and create a structured to-do list to enhance productivity and clarity.

- Foster Regular Communication: Maintaining consistent communication with your team, manager, and clients is paramount. Utilize various channels, such as email, instant messaging, or scheduled video conferences, to ensure seamless connectivity and collaboration.

- Embrace Proactivity: Remote work demands a proactive mindset. Take the initiative in your tasks, don't hesitate to seek assistance when needed, and stay committed to managing your workload efficiently.

- Cultivate Flexibility: In the remote work landscape, plans may occasionally go awry. Embrace adaptability as a core principle, remaining open to unforeseen adjustments and ready to pivot when necessary.

Working remotely offers the allure of a flexible schedule and liberation from the daily commute. By adhering to the tips explained throughout this lesson, you can navigate the realm of remote work with ease, ensuring your career aspirations remain well within reach while maintaining a structured work-life balance.

Haas, M. (2022, February 15). *5 Challenges of Hybrid Work — and How to Overcome Them*. Harvard Business Review. https://hbr.org/2022/02/5-challenges-of-hybrid-work-and-how-to-overcome-them

WORK ON YOUR WRITING

"Anyone and everyone taking a writing class knows the secret of good writing is to cut it back, pare it down, winnow, chop, hack, prune, and trim, remove every superfluous word, compress, compress, compress..."

–Nick Hornby

There are two things you can always improve in your career and never perfect – writing and presenting for business. Like the sport of golf, no one will ever be the perfect writer, but we can all learn from colleagues across every generation. No matter your profession, you will write for the rest of your career so focus on improving your writing for business. While Gen Z has ushered in the use of Slack and text messaging to the workplace, business plans, proposals, thought leadership, emails and many other forms of writing for business will never go out of style. There are outstanding writers at your company across all generations. Proactively seek them out and gain a masterclass in writing for business. Those who excel at writing for business will advance in their careers at a more rapid rate than those who give lip service to writing.

YOU WILL ALWAYS BE PERFECTING YOUR PRESENTATION STYLE

*"You can't stay the same. If you're a musician and
a singer, you have to change, that's the way it works."*

–Van Morrison

Like writing for business, none of us will ever perfect presenting for business. With each presentation, whether to an audience of one or 1,000, we can always improve our delivery. No matter what path your career takes or what industry you enter, you will present to audiences for the next several decades so always attempt to perfect your presentation style knowing you will never reach the finish line. Comprehend that you will present regularly for the next several decades and consider every opportunity you have to speak in front of an audience as an opportunity to refine your delivery. Starting with a job interview, you are making a presentation. It may be one-on-one, but the recipient is judging you based on how you present yourself and whether your delivery is articulate and confident. The more meetings and interviews you schedule, the more comfortable you will become in delivering and communicating your narrative. Once you secure your next job, seek every opportunity to present one-on-one and in a group setting instead of avoiding those opportunities. Along the way, watch how your colleagues across generations present and emulate their best qualities and incorporate those into your delivery. You will never perfect your presentation style, but you will always improve and enhance it if you embrace the fact that presenting to audiences is something that will be a regular part of your career for many years to come.

WORK ON YOUR WEAKNESSES

"My attitude is that if you push me towards something that you think is a weakness, then I will turn that perceived weakness into a strength."

–Michael Jordan

While it is easy to play to your strengths, the greatest opportunity for growth is to work on your weaknesses. No matter where you work, ask your managers and supervisors to provide constructive criticism after your first three, six and 12 months on the job. If you are well established in your career, there is no harm in seeking feedback from colleagues at all levels – millennials, Gen Z, boomers. If there is no formal review process in place, set yourself apart by requesting a review. We all like to hear compliments and praise, but the greatest feedback we can receive is to learn what others perceive as our weaknesses. If you can receive honest feedback on areas for improvement from those who manage you, collaborate with them on setting measurable goals and then work on your weaknesses until you transform them into strengths. Your weaknesses today will be your strengths tomorrow with consistent focus and attention.

LISTEN MORE AND SPEAK LESS

"You can listen to what people say, sure. But you will be far more effective if you listen to what people do."

–Seth Godin

In today's multigenerational workplace, there may be nothing more underrated in business than listening. From questions asked in your first interview to the instructions assigned for your first project, listen carefully and respond accurately. Too often, executives don't listen accurately resulting in a verbal or written response which does not answer the question or the assignment. Take note how senior-level executives who have decades of experience may attend a strategy session and not say a word for the majority of the meeting. Instead, they are actively and accurately listening to everyone's input and analyzing in real-time. After listening closely for the majority of the meeting, they may provide a well-informed point of view based on exactly what the other participants voiced. As you begin your next role, prioritize listening to requests and instructions accurately so that you can deliver a response that is highly effective.

EMBRACE DIVERSITY OF BACKGROUND, EXPERIENCES & THOUGHT

"When everyone is included, everyone wins."

–Reverend Jesse Jackson

In today's multigenerational workplace, there could be colleagues at your company who range in age from 21 (Gen Z) to 81 (Silent Generation) and every age in between. From your first day on the job at your new company and throughout your career, fully embrace diversity of background, experience and thought. Embracing diversity will open your mind to new ideas, opportunities and possibilities you never considered. Imagine if you are a new Gen Z employee who recently graduated college and started your first job at the age of 22 and you have the opportunity to learn from the experiences including failures and lessons from a CEO in their 60s, 70s or 80s. That's a lifetime of learning. What does it mean to embrace diversity? It means having a mindset that seeks and embraces diverse opinions and points of view from individuals who bring different experiences, upbringings, and backgrounds than your own. It is through diverse ideation and problem solving that the greatest solutions will be developed in response to the most daunting business challenges. Throughout your career, when you find yourself standing at the crossroads and have two choices to make, always take the one that will lead to collaboration with the most diverse ideas, insights, and individuals.

OBSERVE OTHERS

*"If you make listening and observation
your occupation you will gain much
more than you can by talk."*

–Robert Baden-Powell

No matter what industry or profession you choose, open your eyes and your ears and be observant at all times whether virtual or in an in-person brainstorm session or presentation. Observing others for positive and even negative habits, routines and practices is something you should be doing every day throughout your career. Take note of best practices from colleagues from all generations and begin to emulate. You can also learn valuable lessons by observing errors, mistakes, and failures. Be a sponge, lift your eyes up from your mobile phone and observe what type of actions and attitudes get a positive reception at whatever company or organization you work. When you are in a meeting (in-person or via virtual meeting platforms), observe how the most effective executives articulate their point-of-view and command respect while other executives spend their time staring at their laptops answering emails or socializing with friends outside the office. It is these types of keen observations that should inspire the way you conduct your business. Never stop observing and learning from your colleagues across all generations.

BALANCE WORK & LIFE

*"Never get so busy making a living that
you forget to make a life."*

–Dolly Parton

Y ou only have one life – don't waste it away by working all the time. Corporations, big and small in today's post-pandemic society, have made it a priority the past several years to ensure that employees are achieving balance in their lives at work and outside of work. More companies are placing a greater emphasis on mental health as Gen Z employees join the workplace and prioritize mental health. In the long run, work-life balance makes us all more effective and productive. As you settle into your new role, be part of a culture that emphasizes a work-life balance. With technology today, we can conduct our work and execute our responsibilities from just about any location in the world. Forward thinking organizations understand that and promote it. One New York-based marketing agency offers their employees six weeks of being a digital nomad. These six weeks are above and beyond vacation days and PTO days. As a digital nomad, employees can work from their favorite beach or mountain. There is no special award for spending the most time in the office or for being the first person on your team to burn out. Remember, success is a marathon, and that means pacing yourself over the next several decades so that you evolve, improve, and become stronger mentally and physically with each passing year. Achieving a work-life balance and inspiring colleagues from all generations to do the same will be incredibly rewarding to you, your colleagues, and the organization you work for.

MENTAL HEALTH MATTERS

*"Mental health... is not a destination, but a process.
It's about how you drive, not where you are going."*

–Noam Shpancer, Ph.D.

Mental health plays a crucial role in the workplace, significantly impacting our ability to work effectively and maintain productivity. One thing that we often forget is the simple fact that we are all humans who share the common trait of having emotions. Now we can agree that we all handle our emotions differently, but the way we handle them can have a positive or negative impact on ourselves and those around us. When we are mentally healthy, we excel at tasks requiring focus, clear thinking, and sound decision-making. Moreover, we become more adept at handling stress and overcoming challenges.

Conversely, poor mental health can lead to several workplace issues, including reduced productivity due to heightened stress or anxiety, increased absenteeism, higher turnover rates, interpersonal conflicts, and potential safety hazards resulting from lapses in judgment. Think back to a time when you are waking up after hearing your alarm, and you lay there, mentally preparing yourself to tackle your day. You understand that you must interact with a teammate or boss, that you really want nothing to do with and would avoid if you could. That emotional discomfort weighs heavily on your mental health, but like everyone else, you must do what you have to do to survive. Remember what you can and cannot control. Should you decide to continue within that environment, do so with a positive mindset. However, if you opt for a different path, remember that your inherent value can be harnessed and appreciated in countless other settings.

An integral aspect of maintaining mental well-being is achieving a work-life balance. On HelpGuide.org, Lawrence Robinson and Melinda Smith stated, "Long hours, understaffing, a lack of support, and harassment in the workplace can ramp up your stress levels and contribute to mental health problems such as anxiety, depression, and substance abuse." It's worth noting that the extent of these challenges varies across professions. Some careers inherently demand more from individuals. It ultimately becomes a matter of choice whether one enters such domains and embraces the associated demands and responsibilities. Nevertheless, achieving equilibrium in the work-life balance equation grants us the precious opportunity to unwind, rejuvenate, and fortify ourselves against the perils of stress and burnout.

Employers play a vital role in fostering mental health in the workplace. They can take several proactive measures, such as providing mental health benefits like therapy and counseling, cultivating a supportive work environment through flexible arrangements and opportunities for socialization, educating employees on mental health matters and destigmatizing discussions around it, and even at some companies, providing flexible paid time off or unlimited PTO. To enhance your mental health while at work, consider the following tips:

- Take Breaks: Regular breaks throughout the day are essential to prevent burnout. Stretch, move around, or step outside for a breath of fresh air.
- Self-Care: Prioritize adequate sleep, a balanced diet, and regular exercise. Physical well-being is closely intertwined with mental health.
- Set Boundaries: Maintain a clear boundary between work and personal life. Avoid checking work emails or taking work-related calls outside of your designated work hours.
- Seek Support: If you're facing mental health challenges, confide in someone you trust, whether it's a friend, family member, or therapist. Talking about your struggles can alleviate stress and provide valuable coping mechanisms.
- Professional Help: Don't hesitate to seek professional assistance if needed. Therapists can help you comprehend your mental health and develop effective coping strategies.

By incorporating these practices, you can enhance your mental well-being and achieve a healthier work-life balance. Your mental health is an invaluable asset and nurturing it through effective self-care is essential. As you continue this journey, you'll find yourself better equipped to navigate the challenges of your career while enjoying a more fulfilling and balanced life. Ultimately, by prioritizing your mental well-being, you're not only enhancing your personal happiness but also fostering the foundation for sustained success.

Mental Health In The Workplace. Help Guide. (n.d.). https://www.helpguide.org/articles/work/mental-health-in-the-workplace.htm

BUILDING EFFECTIVE HABITS

"We are what we repeatedly do. Excellence,
then, is not an act, but a habit."

–Will Durant

By now, you have created a routine that led you to this moment right here. You should be proud of all you have done and the obstacles you've overcome. Because of your relentless work ethic and consistency, you have already won, and your daily habits are the root cause of it all. Habits are the things we do automatically, without thinking. They can be good and bad, and they can have a big impact on our lives. You know this, your family, friends, colleagues, and everyone in between as well. Good habits, which I would like to rename, Effective Habits can help us to be more productive, successful, and happy. Bad habits, also known as, Ineffective Habits, can hold us back and make it difficult to achieve our goals.

In the workplace, effective habits can help us to:

- Be more productive and efficient.
- Meet deadlines and deliver high-quality work.

- Build relationships with colleagues and clients.
- Stay positive and motivated.
- Create a positive work environment.

Ineffective habits can have the opposite effect. They can make us less productive, less efficient, and more stressed. They can also damage our relationships and make it difficult to succeed in our careers. Best-selling author, James Clear, explained it best when he said, "The first mistake is never the one that ruins you. It is the spiral of repeated mistakes that follows. Missing once is an accident. Missing twice is the start of a new habit." That voice in your head that says, "Just do it later. There is always tomorrow", will always be there, but that voice in your head can be your best friend, and your worst enemy when it comes to being productive and efficient.

So, how do we build effective habits? Here are a few tips:

- Start small. Don't try to change too many things at once. Focus on one habit at a time.

- Be specific. What exactly do you want to change? For example, instead of saying "I want to be more organized," say "I want to start filing my paperwork every day."

- Make it easy. Make it as easy as possible to do the new habit. For example, if you want to start exercising, put your workout clothes out the night before.

- Be consistent. The key to building a habit is consistency. Do the new habit every day, even if you don't feel like it.

- Reward yourself. When you stick to the new habit, reward yourself with something you enjoy. This will help you stay motivated.

Building effective habits takes time and effort, but it is worth it. Effective habits can help you to win the job and keep the job, and they can also help you to be more successful in all areas of your life. Here are some specific examples of effective habits that can help you win and keep a job:

- Being punctual and reliable.
- Being organized and efficient.
- Communicating effectively.
- Being proactive and taking initiative.
- Being a team player.
- Being willing to learn and grow.
- Being positive and motivated.

If you can develop these habits, you will be well on your way to continued success. Excellence is a journey, not a destination, as wisely noted by the great Nipsey Hussle, who emphasized experiencing life as a marathon, not a sprint. Staying consistent may pose a challenge, but it's through the execution of effective habits, consistently, that monumental victories are achieved. Uphold your unwavering belief in yourself, and let dedication and motivation be your guiding stars on this remarkable journey and many victory laps to come.

Clear, J. (n.d.). *Atomic Habits Quotes*. James Clear. https://jamesclear.com/quote/atomic-habits

DON'T FORGET TO HAVE FUN

"Just keep taking chances and having fun."

–Garth Brooks

After you have gone through the arduous process of developing your resume, securing an internship, expanding your professional network, conducting rounds of interviews and finally securing your next job, don't forget to have fun. Bob Babbitt is a well-known writer, publisher, podcaster, marketer, promoter – in the endurance sports space, who authored a book titled, "Never A Bad Day." In the introduction, he writes, "Because of the wonderful world of endurance sports and the people who have embraced it, my life has been this awesome journey filled with friends, family, memories and, of course, nothing but great days." Hopefully, all of us can look back on our careers in the same way Bob reflects on his. While you will work hard, you should have fun along the way. No one ever passed a law that said you couldn't have fun while working. When you can pursue your passion and make a career of it like Bob did, there's "never a bad day." As you secure your next job, don't settle just for the paycheck. Instead, consider the fun factor before making your decision. You are joining a company where you will collaborate with colleagues who ages may span 50 years. That alone offers an opportunity for a fun and enriching experience.

PAY FORWARD WHAT
YOU LEARNED

"When you get where you're goin'
Don't forget turn back around
Help the next one in line
Always stay humble and kind"

–Tim McGraw

Remember earlier statements in this book on building that emotional bank account when you network. We tell everyone that we help that their network is the only rainy-day insurance policy any of us have when, and if, we find ourselves in a job search. Therefore, continue to network each day even as you work in your full-time role. Help everyone you can across all generations – Gen Z, millennials, Gen X, baby boomers, Silent Generation - when you come across those in need. Your help can be everything from referring them to a networking group and accepting their LinkedIn connection to endorsing their skills and writing a recommendation letter to serving as a reference and helping them with their resume and running them through a mock interview. "I will never say no to helping someone in need no matter how busy or occupied I might be," said PJ Brovak, a marketing communications veteran. "I am thankful for the hundreds, yes hundreds, of people who invested their time in me. And I always tell those individuals I help that you never know when I might need to call on them in the future for some reason." If we live our lives by consistently making daily deposits into the emotional bank account with those who we encounter and grow and nurture relationships with those contacts, we will each be rewarded with a stronger network that will be there for us when we need it most. Brovak added, "And when you hear of the success that someone has had and realize that you might have played even just a small part of it, there is not a more rewarding feeling." In today's multigenerational workforce, there is nothing more fulfilling.

BONUS SECTION

Employment Campaign – Military To Civilian Transition
By Don Weyler, U.S. Army Lieutenant Colonel (Retired)

Introduction: As this is the military to civilian transition portion of this book, let me tell my transition story in the "war story" language my military family can relate to best: "So there I was..." concluding a 22-year career in the Army. I had the great honor and pleasure to start my career as a logistics officer, right out of college. I had opportunities to lead organizations, support operations and plan and execute process improvements to provide the best possible support to our service members in combat, peace keeping operations and here in the US. During that career, I learned that the military is a great leadership laboratory and provides service members with a career map of various options to advance careers and provide maximum value to their respective service. As I began the transition to a civilian career, I realized that unlike the military, there is not one cohesive map. There is not a clear direction. The transition can be daunting. In fact, it could be your next "War story", but it doesn't have to be.

Lessons Learned: The origin of this chapter began as I drafted my own lessons learned and some techniques, tactics, and procedures I picked up along the way. I did not enjoy the job hunt, but eventually, I was successful in landing a senior leadership position in a Fortune 50 Company. My intent was to pass on these lessons learned with many of the great friends I have met over the years and many veterans I have volunteered to assist. While written in an organized fashion, I will not lie to you and tell you I was anywhere near this organized as I transitioned to my civilian career. I am not going to tell you that this is a comprehensive guide to tell you everything as you transition. There are many resources to provide great insight to subjects you will need to learn for the next steps: Elevator pitches, Resumes, Cover letters, dealing with Applicant Candidate Tracking Systems (ATS), etc. While we will touch on these subjects, this is more of a checklist to keep you organized as you move on to the next phase in your life. I hope you find this outline to be helpful and I wish you the very best in your future. Thank you for your service!

Challenges At The Outset: When I started my employment campaign, I discovered I had three major challenges:

1. Career Direction: I wasn't entirely sure of what I wanted to do in my next career. I wanted to be challenged. I wanted to be away from the Department of Defense. That was my initial direction.

2. Translating my military skills into civilian speak. I didn't know how to articulate my value proposition for a company. "I managed a $7.7 Billion dollar budget and was chief of operations for a 2,000 Soldier organization." – "So what?" they responded. Yes, a little deflating.

3. Networking – It is really hard to enter a cold, new world and meet new folks and ask for help. If entering a new industry, the challenge is figuring out what questions to ask. Military to military, we are used to collaborating and supporting a common cause. Additionally, we speak our own language – or speak "shorthand" as I explained to a civilian boss of mine. When dealing with a new audience, do not assume they have any understanding of what you have done or how you do it.

This Employment Campaign Plan is organized into Five Phases: To overcome these challenges, I stumbled into a five-phase solution which can help you in your transition. While written sequentially, some of these phases may occur concurrently:

Phase I Early Phase: Focus your efforts prior to transition:

- Changing your mindset: As service members, we think we can do anything, as such, sometimes we are not overly focused on our next steps when it comes time to career transition. "I will do anything with a good company that can let me use my strengths to their benefit, in a role I enjoy and pays nicely!" While this flexibility is a great military trait, what you will find is this approach handcuffs you, as you will see later when we discuss building targeted resumes (More to follow in Phase II). It also limits you when you meet and network with people. Everyone wants to help a service member in transition, but if they don't know what support you need and you can't articulate WHAT opportunities you are looking for, these supporters can and will do very little until you have sorted this out. (More to follow in Phase III).

- Start to define what you want to do in your next life: I recommend you get a book called "What's Next" by Ruehlin Associates. It is a very good book on the military to civilian transition. If you are not firmly rooted in your next career, purchase books such as "What Color is my Parachute?" and check out your personality type on humanmetrics.com. It is free and after you take the Jung personality test, it will give you career choices best suited to your personality. Did I mention this service is free?

- TAP: Make sure you do the Transition Assistance Program (TAP), especially the Department of Labor employment seminar portion. It provides you with a list of resources and links to further inform your job hunt. For field grades and more senior leaders, it is recommended you attend a TAP event at either the Army War College at Carlisle, PA or the National War College at Fort McNair, as they will have the ability to cater a little more to senior folks.

- Civilian Certifications: Start working now to leverage your services e-learning platforms to bolster your military skills into easier to understand "Civilian Certifications." Recommend you research "Project Management Professional" at PMI.org. You can take all the pre-requisites for free, then pay $400 for the PMP certification. Corporate America often pays 10K in bonuses to managers that have this. Another one to take advantage of is Lean Six Sigma. Take any "process improvement" qualifications you can get. Most military folks spend their lives doing process improvement, but most civilians haven't a clue that we do continually look to improve our operations and expand our competitive advantage. Maximize those civilian certifications. APICS, TQM, etc. - Veterans Affairs and your retirement/ transition physical: Make sure you get all your ailments seen. Ensure you get three documented appointments for every ailment. Document it. Also, google the BDD - Benefits Delivered on Discharge. You can start your VA claim 6 months out. Ensure you get your retirement physical scheduled prior to that so you can get the BDD completed. You want to clear these items up as you prepare to transition so you can be focused on your next career. Start as early as possible and get these administrative requirements out of the way so you can begin Phase II activities!

Phase II Translating your Skills- Defining your Value Proposition

- Resumes! Develop your Master List of Awesomeness – called a Base Resume: Write everything down in bullet format from your evaluations. For instance – "Accountable for a 10 million budget." SO what? Well, if it said, "Achieved cost saving of 20 percent while managing a $10 million budget." THAT would speak to someone hiring. A base resume is good to have as you can mix and match the bullets, in order to give the audience (hiring manager/HR team) what they want.

- Basics: Only go back 10 years and write down all the magnificent things from your evaluations in reverse chronological order. Write them in such a way that it shows "what you did for the enterprise." Bullets must pass the "so what" test. Basically, it represents the Cause and Effect of your professionalism.

- PARs/CARs - You aren't done when you pull together all of those bullets. Next you must use PARs/CARs. It was vital to rewrite the resume in the Problem Action Result/Challenge Action Result format. This is hard to do, because as a job seeker, we generally don't want to leave anything out and some of those bullets, imported from your Master List of Awesomeness, will need to go. Getting your ego out of the resume writing is a challenge worth overcoming. PARs/CARs are story telling. It puts your most important accomplishments in context. It paints the picture vs. a list of unrelated, but impressive accomplishments. You must use the PARs/CARs in order to develop your "value proposition" (what talents, skills and abilities you bring to the position for your potential employer to consider.) Next, ensure your PARs/CARs are bucketed by category so you can pull them as needed to make a compelling case for your future employment.

- Formulate Different Types of Resumes – Using your PARs/CARs pull bullets and smoosh them into different resumes for different functions. This works well if you are looking at various occupations and industries (Operations vs. Training & Development, Project Management vs. HR). Pull them out of those evaluations and bucket them by functional area.

- Cover Letters - I thought the resume was the big kahuna, but it seemed like cover letters are everything: Even when you apply on portals. If possible, get the name of the HR or the hiring manager so you can personally address the letter. When possible, I prefer to use the T- letter. The T-letter works like so: on one side, stating what they are looking for (directly from job announcement or posting) and on the other column, your skills, experience, and qualifications to demonstrate that you meet or exceed that qualification. This is one of the best ways to highlight your value proposition.

- Once you feel comfortable that you have a decent base resume, review your resume with your friends, family, and contacts who will speak the truth to you about what you have written. Continue to work and refine your product and then you are ready for Phase III.

Phase III Building the Network – Intelligence Gathering

- The 30-second Elevator Pitch: Before you attend any networking group, have in mind your 30-second elevator pitch. Realize that anyone you meet could be a potential employer. Rehearse and have an elevator speech in your head..."I am _____. I am transitioning out of the military after a successful XX-year career leading teams in Y countries AND..." Be ready with what industries/companies/locations you are targeting. In the military, we tend to think we can do anything/everything, but if you aren't specific when you meet people, they don't know how to help you with your transition.

- Networking: Leverage LinkedIn to find veteran's groups in the community you want to transition to. They can be the window to employment. Get to be part of networking groups, both veteran and professional. (Go to landingexpert.com to get a list of networking groups for professions, locations, etc. It is a free pdf download). Additionally, there are lots of local veteran groups you can find on LinkedIn. (See additional resources links at the conclusion of this opus) I found the Great Philadelphia Networking Group to be very helpful in putting vets in contact with other vets. Go to LinkedIn and search. Join the Breakfast Club of NJ at thebreakfastclubofnj.com. Even if you don't settle in this area, their website is priceless with all the different references and articles which were an invaluable resource as I transitioned. The meetings are currently still remote post Covid, free to join and are the second Saturday of each month at 8 am ET.

- Informational Interviews: Early on, I recommend if you have an idea of a role, a company or type of industry you would like to pursue, I recommend you leverage informational interviews. You may find out the company you wanted to be a part of does not meet your expectations, or you may get great insight on how to shape your resume, LinkedIn profile and 30-second elevator pitch.

- Professional Associations: Join them. Look into the Military Officers Association of America (MOAA) and join. They have employment seminars, and you can hang a resume in their portal. They give some free resume advice. If you want to go corporate, join American Corporate Partners - it is an organization that recruits employees from numerous Fortune 500 companies to act as mentors for transitioning service members. IN this program, you will be someone's mentee for a year. It is not a hiring program, but the mentors can help you shape your own employment campaign and the assistance and support is free. There are a lot of other free resources which I will include at the end of the chapter.

- Wardrobe: Meetings: The War College has a seminar, "Dress for Success," which tells you how to dress for interviews as a civilian. Some of it is common sense. Some of it is ridiculous, but just when you think it is silly, you run into that fellow officer wearing his corfams and the belt from his service uniform for a job interview and you think..." Hmmmm. Maybe we do need this?"

- Business Cards: I recommend that you get business cards and a professional looking portfolio for job fairs to carry resumes and business cards. The Army green notebook is not what you need! Ensure you have these civilian business cards when you get closer to transitioning.

- LinkedIn: Build a profile on LinkedIn. Have a photo. Make it look like a more detailed version of your 30-second pitch, with some compelling facts about you. Ensure as you get closer – use the term "TRANSITIONING

MILITARY" over "Retiring." Nobody wants to hire someone who is retired. They think you will have no fire. Additional pointers: put SEEKING AND AVAILABLE for employment in either your title or your current company field. HR and Recruiters routinely do searches...I got three job interviews alone out of random LinkedIn searches).

- Following these initial LinkedIn tasks, use LinkedIn to build your network within a company. I targeted HR folks in my target companies. They can be a gateway in, but you really want the HIRING MANAGER or to get someone who knows the hiring manager.

- Social Media: Get accounts on glassdoor.com, indeed. com, clearance jobs.com. Don't apply through those sites, but see what is open where, and try to go to the specific company and apply. Better yet, target someone on LinkedIn, and work through them as well. BEST YET – Leverage your networking to get to a hiring manager.

Then move onto Facebook/Instagram and be very careful what you post. Don't post opinions because all Human Resources and recruiting types will google you and see your social media profiles. Rules of thumb: Political opinions, images of your partying... well, anything that makes you look like less of a responsible citizen as you work your job hunt should NOT be posted. You can go back to posting that stuff AFTER you are hired...unless you sign an ethics clause...or something.

Phase IV Interviews: The End is Near and so is the new beginning:

- Job interviews. Never say "Retired military", say "Transitioning," or else they might think you are going to come in and coast. Also, all those excellent bullets you thought of for the resume, plan to develop stories that are tight and focused, put them in a "STAR" format - Situation, Task, Action, Result. All the war stories we have are there, just have them kicking in your head for the interview.

- Interviewing – After about a half dozen interviews and dwindling job prospects, it started to hit me that I stunk at interviews. But, after listening to all the great speakers at networking groups, I put in the work for the interviews. What worked for me is(was) getting copies of "the 101 most challenging interview questions" then developing answers for all of them in a STAR or SHARE format – Situation Task Action Result or Situation Hindrance Action Result Evaluation. Then reading / rehearsing the answers, so(until) they come out naturally during the interview.

- Questions: Make sure YOU have questions. Not about vacation or bonuses, but how the role fits into the big picture. Ideas of what hiring manager thinks "success" looks like, ideas of how the role will develop, how the company will evolve etc. Answers you get to these questions feed into your ...THANK YOU NOTES.

- Thank You Notes: Hand write them. Send them IMMEDIATELY. Ensure you mention some aspect of the interview, so they know you were paying attention and how you are uniquely talented to solve that problem. Email is mandatory as well. Ensure the email and the thank you note refer to something the hiring manager stated in the interview, but make sure the email and thank you note don't say exactly the same thing.

- Leverage your networking groups for – entry points into the companies, interviewing help, advice on how to best utilize recruiters. The services provided by most of these groups are FREE. Most of these groups are run by volunteers who are working and want to pay forward and support others as they themselves have been through the job hunt. Another benefit is that it is good to hear from others who have landed their next position and what worked for them. It is always good to learn from other people and catch their spin on the job campaign.

- Portals: If you applied on a portal, ensure you have copies of your answers to their screening questions, the cover letter, the resume you submitted and the job notice. Yes, this sounds like common sense, but I applied to over 110 jobs, and got calls months after I saw the position had closed. Fortunately, after I did not get hired in the first few months, I began a rudimentary tracking system and began saving all my submissions. I missed a few early in my job hunt!

- Track your submissions: See above.

Phase V Landing:

- Networking: Once you have landed, you must continue to network within the company. Being totally brand new to the civilian work force, it is good to have contacts in your business unit but ideally you will also want contacts outside your business unit, to bounce questions, get opinions and put things into context. Corporate cultures can be hard to get used to: Do meetings start on time? Do you bring your computer to meetings? Telework?

How do I navigate time off? Dress Codes, etc. All these things that can make you panic the night before a day in the office.

- Employee Resource Groups: Many large companies have ERGs. Most have Veteran Leadership Councils or similar internal organizations. These are good opportunities to meet with people in your company from other business units and build that company network. Find people with similar backgrounds who may have gone through and met some of the challenges you will encounter in your new role. The more contacts the better. In my experience, most people, if they can assist and know what you need, they will assist.

Other Resources:

Military Resources on LinkedIn: There are many military transition organizations out there. All free. If they are charging, go somewhere else. Most of these organizations are focused on military to corporate transfer vs. government. Off the top of my head and groups you can access from LinkedIn:

American Corporate Partners: I was a protegee then a mentor of three transitioning SMs when I was with J&J.

Military MOJO: They run quarterly job fair/meet and greet with transition service members and Fortune 500 companies.

Hire Military, Michael Quinn: A retired CSM and bigtime LinkedIn Influencer runs this organization.

4Block: They are a group that has classes for numerous veterans transitioning and takes them around to Corp America to teach them about transition. They have an extensive curriculum and are in a few cities on the east coast.

Military to Government Transition – A Few Points:

- The resume is really pretty ugly.
  - You literally break most of the rules for civilian resumes and have the key words pulled directly from the job announcement.
  - Then, with a sentence from your career saying how you accomplished that particular thing.
  - To ensure you get selected, and you break all the civilian resume rules, write using their exact wording of duties, and then write your experience executing said duties.

Good Luck, Don!

About Don Weyler: Don is a retired Army Lieutenant Colonel who had the distinct honor and pleasure to serve as a logistics officer. Over the next 22 years, Don had the great fortune to travel and perform in several leadership positions from logistics platoon leader to two company commands, finally culminating as a two-time Brigade Deputy Commander, or the second in command of organizations of over 2,000 Soldiers. He was proud to provide support to Infantry, Aviation and Special Forces units in assignments in Korea, Fort Bragg, North Carolina, Germany, Italy, Egypt, Fort Lee, Virginia and three tours in Afghanistan. After retirement, Don originally transitioned to Corporate America, where he worked as a Director of Global Operations and later as a Chief of Staff in a global supply chain. After his time in Corporate America, Don transitioned back and is currently working for the Department of Defense as a Chief of Logistics Plans and Programs.

FINAL THOUGHTS

As this book highlights consistently, the workplace has transformed significantly since the arrival of the pandemic in 2020. Long gone are the days of reporting to a physical office five days a week. With change comes challenges and opportunities. This book is intended to help each individual job seeker overcome career challenges and fully leverage opportunities.

We hope that as you transform and evolve in your career, you gain value from the lessons, recommendations, and advice that the three authors offer in this book. No matter what stage you are at in your career, there is information and content in this book that will help you successfully navigate your unique career journey.

This book is just one valuable piece of your career puzzle that also includes family, friends, colleagues, classmates, recruiters, career networking support groups and people who you have not met yet who are all eager to support you as you aspire to write the next chapter in your career.

From the three authors of this book, we wish you the very best of success in securing your next job and even greater success once you start that new job and thrive in your new role!

ABOUT THE AUTHORS

Mark Beal

For more than 25 years, Mark Beal served as a public relations practitioner and marketer for one of the nation's leading consumer public relations agencies developing and executing marketing and public relations campaigns for leading companies and brands around such major sports and entertainment properties as the Olympic Games, Super Bowl, World Series, US Open Tennis and The Rolling Stones.

Today, he collaborates with Gen Z as a full-time professor of practice, communication in the Rutgers University School of Communication and Information. Mark's ongoing research of Gen Z has led to keynote speeches to the American Marketing Association, Association of National Advertisers (ANA) and the Public Relations Society of America (PRSA)

It was Mark's Rutgers students who inspired him to author his first book in 2017, *101 Lessons They Never Taught You In College*, which provides tips to college students preparing for their transition to a career. Media and readers nationwide responded so positively to the book that Mark authored *101 Lessons They Never Taught You In High School About Going To College* which was published in 2018.

Mark's book, *Decoding Gen Z: 101 Lessons Generation Z Will Teach Corporate America, Marketers & Media*, was published in 2018 and captured the attention of media, marketers and employers nationwide as Gen Zers were starting to become a focus of corporations and brands. In 2020, Mark co-authored *Engaging Gen Z* with Harvard University student Michael Pankowski. In 2022, Mark authored *Gen Z Graduates To Adulthood*. Mark's latest book, *ZEO*, was published in 2023 as more Gen Zers transitioned from college to their career. The Gen Z books have led to invitations from conferences, corporations, brands, agencies, universities, industry associations and pro sports leagues and teams for Mark to deliver keynote speeches featuring his Gen Z research and insights.

Mark also co-authored *Career In Transition* with Frank Kovacs.

To learn more, visit www.markbealspeaks.com.

ABOUT THE AUTHORS

Frank Kovacs

Frank Kovacs has been a technology business executive for more than 30 years leading and directing large, complex, global operations and transformations for some of the largest Fortune 100 firms as well as NASA.

Frank has been recognized as recipient of the Gartner CIO Choice Award, Visionary Award from Business Finance Magazine & Internet World, and the Ovation Award at Comnet. Frank was named a visionary for his 12 years of work at AT&T Bell Labs and has a patent for Smart Card Technology.

Following the attacks of September 11, 2001, Frank wanted to help those who lost their jobs due to the tragedy and formed a group, The Breakfast Club NJ (TBCNJ). More than 18 years later, TBCNJ has grown to more than 6,000 members and is the premier job search and career networking group in the New York/New Jersey region. As TBCNJ extensively leverages social media, many of the job posts and career transition advice routinely go viral and TBCNJ has helped more than 9,000 individuals secure jobs all with a "pay-it-forward" volunteer approach.

Frank is very proud to capture many of the learnings from 18 years of TBCNJ and share them through this book in hopes that even more people will be helped with their respective job search as we all work through the challenges of today's digital disruption and reskilling.

Frank is a lifelong resident of South River and East Brunswick, New Jersey where he lives with his wife, Laurie, daughter, Julianna, and their German Shepherd, Rubie.

ABOUT THE AUTHORS

Kadeer A. Porter

Kadeer is a dynamic individual who has seamlessly blended his lifelong dedication to martial arts with a remarkable journey in the world of business and sports. From his early days at the age of 4, Kadeer immersed himself in the world of martial arts, going on to excel in high-level competitions at both local and regional levels, end even reaching the pinnacle of achievement at the USA Taekwondo Junior Olympics.

As a first-generation graduate, Kadeer combined his passion for martial arts with his business acumen, ultimately earning a master's degree in global sports business from Rutgers University in New Jersey. During his time in the program, he played a pivotal role in establishing the inaugural Mayweather Boxing and Fitness facility in the state.

After receiving his master's degree in Global Sports Business from Rutgers University, Kadeer delved into the realm of talent acquisition, joining the ranks of On Locations, a prominent company under the Endeavor umbrella. His role involved crafting teams at the highest echelons of sports, hospitality, and entertainment, collaborating with renowned entities like the IOC, NFL, NCAA, UFC, WWE, MLB, PGA Tour/Ryder

Cup, NASCAR, PBR, 160over90, YouTube Fest and Coachella. Kadeer's ability to connect with people on a personal level, backed by his profound emotional intelligence, proved to be a cornerstone of his success as a Corporate Recruiter within the industry.

With his finger on the pulse of emerging technologies and the constantly evolving landscape of inclusive industries, Kadeer is a passionate advocate for disseminating this critical knowledge. He stands poised to empower individuals with the skills and wisdom needed to navigate the complex world of job hunting, leveraging his diverse experiences to pave the way for others to achieve their dreams.